THE

PIZZA TASTES GREAT

WORKBOOK

SECOND EDITION

WILLIAM P. PICKETT

Longman

To My Mother and Father

The Pizza Tastes Great Workbook, Second Edition

Pearson Education, 10 Bank Street, White Plains, NY 10606

Vice president, director of instructional design: Allen Ascher
Acquisitions editor: Laura Le Dréan
Development director: Penny Laporte
Development editor: Paula H. Van Ells
Vice president, director of design and production: Rhea Banker
Associate director of electronic production: Aliza Greenblatt
Executive managing editor: Linda Moser
Production manager: Ray Keating
Associate production editor: Corrie Sublett-Berríos
Director of manufacturing: Patrice Fraccio
Senior manufacturing buyer: Edie Pullman
Cover design adaptation: Monika Popowitz
Associate digital layout manager: Paula D. Williams
Text art: Don Martinetti

ISBN: 0-13-041391-7

4 5 6 7 8 9 10-BAH-07 06 05

Contents

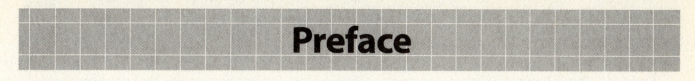

Preface

Purpose

The purpose of *The Pizza Tastes Great Workbook* is to increase a student's reading, speaking, listening, and writing skills. The exercises in the workbook also reinforce and expand the vocabulary of *The Pizza Tastes Great*. The exercises give students an opportunity to work with others and on their own, sometimes reviewing the dialogs and stories of *The Pizza Tastes Great*, and sometimes using new material.

New in the Second Edition

A Word Bank has been added before all the dialogs of *The Pizza Tastes Great Workbook*. The dialogs and stories have been revised to make them clearer, more interesting, and up-to-date. Two new dialogs have been added.

Content

All eight chapters of *The Pizza Tastes Great Workbook* begin with a review section. This section consists of true-false questions to check the student's comprehension of a dialog or story of the student book, and sentence-completion exercises to test and reinforce the vocabulary of the student book.

A dialog or story follows the review section. The dialogs are patterned on the dialogs of the student book, but feature new ideas and new vocabulary. They are preceded by a Word Bank that defines or explains the more difficult words in the dialog. After the students complete the dialog, they either write one of their own or they interview another student. When writing their own dialogs, the students use the dialogs of both the student book and the workbook as models. The stories in the workbook are shorter than those in the student book and are meant to be read and enjoyed, and to serve as models for student compositions.

Each lesson, therefore, progresses from a review section to a dialog or story, to sections in which students apply what they have learned by writing their own dialog or story or by interviewing other students. This gives students the opportunity to be creative and to express their own ideas. The language they produce will be imperfect, but their self-activity will help develop confidence and an ability to use English independently.

Use

The exercises in this workbook can be used immediately after finishing a dialog or story in *The Pizza Tastes Great*, or they can be used after completing a chapter. Students can use the workbook in class and at home.

Word List and Answer Key

There is a word list at the end of the workbook. It includes the words used in the word-review exercises, the dialogs, and the matching exercises. A separate booklet contains an answer key to *The Pizza Tastes Great* and to this workbook.

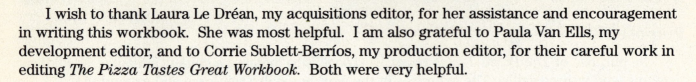

Acknowledgments

I wish to thank Laura Le Dréan, my acquisitions editor, for her assistance and encouragement in writing this workbook. She was most helpful. I am also grateful to Paula Van Ells, my development editor, and to Corrie Sublett-Berríos, my production editor, for their careful work in editing *The Pizza Tastes Great Workbook*. Both were very helpful.

The art work of Don Martinetti has captured the spirt of the dialogs and has added much to the workbook. I thank him for his lively illustrations.

Above all, I am grateful to my wife, Dorothy, for her thorough review of the workbook and her many valuable suggestions.

WP

1

Food

A Good Cook

Reread the dialog "A Good Cook" (page 3 of **The Pizza Tastes Great**) before doing the dialog and word reviews.

DIALOG REVIEW

*If the sentence is true, write **T**. If it's false, write **F** and change it to a true statement.*

1. _____ Amy's dad is in the living room.
   _____

2. _____ He's cooking dinner.
   _____

3. _____ His wife is talking on the phone.
   _____

4. _____ She's tired.
   _____

5. _____ Amy's dad always cooks.
   _____

6. _____ He's a good cook.
   _____

WORD REVIEW

Complete the sentences with these words.

where's	kitchen	cook	dinner

1. I'm hungry. Is _____ ready?
2. The cat is in the _____.
3. _____ my hat?
4. My mom likes to _____.

always	living room	watching	tired

5. I'm _____. I want to sit down.
6. I _____ wash my hands before I eat.
7. Who is _____ the baby?
8. Scott is in the _____. He's sitting on the sofa.

ON THE CELL PHONE

WORD BANK

A **cell phone** is a phone that people carry with them.
The **dining room** is the room in which you eat.

Complete the dialog with these words and practice it with a partner.

dining room	much	mom	cell phone	all	reading

Wing is Lee's girlfriend. They're at Lee's home.

Wing: Where's your _____?

 Lee: In the living room.

Wing: What's she doing?

 Lee: _____ the newspaper.

Wing: Where's your dad?

 Lee: In the _____.

Wing: What's he doing?

 Lee: Talking on the _____.

Wing: Is he on the phone _____?

 Lee: Yes, _____ the time.

WRITING A DIALOG

Work with a partner and create your own dialog. Give your dialog a title.

_____

A: Where's _____?

B: She's _____.

A: What's she doing?

B: _____

A: _____

B: _____

A: _____

B: _____

ROOMS IN A HOME

Work with a partner and list as many rooms as you can that are in a home. Then list two or more things you see in them.

Rooms	Things in Them
1. _____	_____
2. _____	_____
3. _____	_____
4. _____	_____
5. _____	_____
6. _____	_____
7. _____	_____

To the Supermarket

Reread the dialog "To the Supermarket" (page 6 of **The Pizza Tastes Great**) before doing the dialog and word reviews.

DIALOG REVIEW

If the sentence is true, write **T**. If it's false, write **F** and change it to a true statement.

1. _____ The car keys are on the dining room table.

   _____

2. _____ Maya is going to the bank.

   _____

3. _____ Maya and Jamal eat a lot.

   _____

4. _____ Maya wants Jamal to go with her.

   _____

5. _____ He's busy.

   _____

6. _____ The packages will be heavy.

   _____

WORD REVIEW

Complete the sentences with these words.

can	if	again	key

1. Where is the _____ to the cabinet?

2. _____ you speak Spanish?

3. Say it _____.

4. _____ you're going to lunch, I'll go with you.

packages	a lot	heavy	busy

5. Henry talks _____.

6. Put the _____ on the table.

7. Is the store _____ on Saturday morning?

8. The desk is _____.

5

BASEBALL IN THE PARK

WORD BANK
Another means one more person or thing. A **cap** is a hat. Baseball players wear caps. A **park** is a place where people go to walk or play. **Too** means also.

Complete the dialog with these words and practice it with a partner.

play	cap	another	thanks	too	park

Tony and Bill are friends. They like to play baseball.

Tony: Did you see my baseball _____?

Bill: It's on the TV.

Tony: You're right. _____.

Bill: Where are you going?

Tony: To the _____.

Bill: Again?

Tony: Yes. I love to _____ baseball.

Bill: Can I go with you?

Tony: Sure you can.

Bill: I like to play baseball _____.

Tony: Good. We can use _____ player.

INTERVIEWING

Ask a partner these questions.

1. May I ask you some questions?
2. Do you like to talk on the phone?
3. Do you ever call another country? Which country? How often do you call there?
4. Do you like baseball?
5. Do you ever watch it on TV? How often?
6. Do you have a team you like very much? If you do, what team?
7. Do they play baseball in your country? Do they play very much?
8. The United States loves baseball. Can you name two other countries that love baseball?

WHAT I LIKE TO DO

List some things you like to do.

1. I like to _____.

2. I like to _____.

3. I like to _____.

4. I like to _____.

5. I like to _____.

PLACES I GO

List some places you go.

1. I go to _____.

2. I go to _____.

3. I go to _____.

4. I go to _____.

5. I go to _____.

A Little Milk but No Sugar

Reread the dialog "A Little Milk but No Sugar" (page 9 of **The Pizza Tastes Great**) before doing the dialog and word reviews.

DIALOG REVIEW

If the sentence is true, write **T**. If it's false, write **F** and change it to a true statement.

1. _____ Megan wants a cup of coffee.
   _____

2. _____ She asks for a little milk and sugar.
   _____

3. _____ Eric frequently drinks coffee at night.
   _____

4. _____ Coffee keeps him awake.
   _____

5. _____ Tea helps him relax.
   _____

6. _____ Megan loves tea.
   _____

WORD REVIEW

Complete the sentences with these words.

at night	never	please	something

1. I have _____ to give you.

2. _____ listen to me.

3. Igor doesn't like to drive _____.

4. Rachel _____ goes to the movies.

little	relax	awake	keeps

5. Stay _____ in class!

6. The air conditioning _____ the room cool.

7. At night, I like to watch TV and _____.

8. May I have a _____ more ice cream?

I LOVE CAKE

<table>
<tr><th colspan="2">WORD BANK</th></tr>
</table>

Dessert is food you eat after dinner, for example, ice cream, cake, and pie.
A **piece** is a part of something.
Too means more than is good or necessary.

Complete the dialog with these words and practice it with a partner.

any	dessert	like	piece	too	chocolate

Sara is visiting Matt. They're cousins.

Matt: Would you _____ something to drink?

Sara: A cup of hot _____, please.

Matt: And a _____ of cake?

Sara: Sure, I love cake.

Matt: I do too, but I can't have _____.

Sara: Why not?

Matt: I'm _____ heavy.

Sara: What do you eat for _____?

Matt: An apple or an orange.

Sara: I never have fruit for dessert.

WRITING A DIALOG

Work with a partner and create your own dialog. Give your dialog a title.

_____

A: Would you like something to drink?

B: _____, please.

A: And _____?

B: Sure, I _____.

A: _____

B: _____

A: _____

B: _____

DRINKS, DESSERTS, FRUITS

Work with a partner and try to list eight drinks, desserts, and fruits. Put a check (✓) after those that you like a lot.

	Drinks	Desserts	Fruits
1.	_____	_____	_____
2.	_____	_____	_____
3.	_____	_____	_____
4.	_____	_____	_____
5.	_____	_____	_____
6.	_____	_____	_____
7.	_____	_____	_____
8.	_____	_____	_____

A Big Menu

Reread the dialog "A Big Menu" (page 12 of **The Pizza Tastes Great**) before doing the dialog and word reviews.

DIALOG REVIEW

*If the sentence is true, write **T**. If it's false, write **F** and change it to a true statement.*

1. _____ The restaurant has a small menu.
   _____

2. _____ Brian is getting turkey, peas, and mashed potatoes.
   _____

3. _____ The fish at the restaurant isn't good.
   _____

4. _____ Kristin had fish yesterday.
   _____

5. _____ She gets roast beef and mashed potatoes.
   _____

6. _____ She likes carrots.
   _____

WORD REVIEW

Complete the sentences with these words.

menu	getting	roast beef	vegetables

1. I'm _____ soup and a salad for lunch.

2. Eat your _____! They're good for you.

3. Waiter! May I have a _____, please?

4. I don't want turkey. I'm going to have _____.

fish	perfect	how about	mashed potatoes

5. _____ a hot dog and french fries?

6. I'm making a tuna _____ sandwich.

7. The _____ are cold.

8. No one is _____.

CHICKEN AND RICE

WORD BANK
Excellent means very good. An **idea** is a thought or plan. When you think, you get *ideas*. To **order** is to ask for the food you want at a restaurant. **Ready** means prepared to do something.

Complete the dialog with these words and practice it with a partner.

yesterday	idea	order	excellent	how about	ready

Emily is Nick's girlfriend. They're eating in a nice restaurant.

Emily: This is a pretty restaurant.

Nick: Yes, and the food is _____.

Emily: Are you _____ to order?

Nick: Yes. I'm getting steak, french fries, and a salad.

Emily: I don't know what to _____.

Nick: They have very good Italian food.

Emily: I know, but I had spaghetti _____.

Nick: _____ chicken?

Emily: Good _____. I'll get chicken and rice.

Nick: And what vegetable do you want?

Emily: Broccoli, if they have it.

INTERVIEWING

Ask a partner these questions.

1. May I ask you some questions?

2. What do you drink at breakfast? And at dinner?

3. Do you like hot chocolate? Do you drink a lot of it?

4. Do you like spaghetti?

5. Do you like pizza?

6. Do you eat much chicken? Rice?

7. What do you eat more often—rice or potatoes?

8. Do you like steak? Do you eat it often?

COMPLETING A STORY

Work with a partner and write your own story. Give your story a title.

_____

My wife and I are eating dinner at a restaurant. We are looking at the _____.

My wife is getting _____.

And I'm getting _____.

My wife is going to have _____ for dessert, but I'm not getting any

dessert because _____.

My wife loves to eat at restaurants because _____

_____, but we don't eat out much because

_____.

The Pizza Tastes Great

Reread the story "The Pizza Tastes Great" (page 15 of **The Pizza Tastes Great***) before doing the Story Review, Word Review, and Word and Story Review.*

STORY REVIEW

If the sentence is true, write **T**. *If it's false, write* **F** *and change it to a true statement.*

1. _____ Dave works fast.

   _____

2. _____ He's frequently late.

   _____

3. _____ Michelle walks and talks slowly.

   _____

4. _____ She's frequently early.

   _____

5. _____ Dave likes pizza and ice cream.

   _____

6. _____ Michelle never eats cake or candy.

   _____

7. _____ She never thinks about her weight.

   _____

WORD REVIEW

Complete the sentences with these words.

fast	so	diet	pounds

1. I'm _____ tired. I can't stay awake.

2. & 3. Dan weighs 250 _____. He's on a _____.

4. Paula reads _____.

14

only	careful	worry	different

5. When my husband is late, I _____ about him.

6. These shoes are _____ $40.

7. Juan and Ricardo are good friends, but they go to _____ schools.

8. Sandra is a good doctor. She's very _____.

WORD AND STORY REVIEW

Complete the dialog with these words and practice it with a partner.

late	thin	living room	calories
favorite	early	weigh	always

Eating Ice Cream

Dave is in the living room reading and eating ice cream. Michelle wants to know what he's doing. They're going to a party tonight.

Michelle: Where are you?

Dave: In the _____.

Michelle: What are you doing?

Dave: Reading the newspaper and eating ice cream.

Michelle: You're _____ eating ice cream.

Dave: Well, it's my _____ food.

Michelle: I know. That's why you _____ so much.

Dave: And why are you so _____?

Michelle: I eat a lot of fish and vegetables.

Dave: And you never eat ice cream and cake.

Michelle: That's because they have a lot of _____.

Dave: What time is the party tonight?

Michelle: Nine o'clock. We're leaving at eight-fifteen.

Dave: Why so _____?

Michelle: I don't want to be _____.

Dave: OK, early bird. I'll be ready.

READING A STORY

Read the story about Alex and Sam. They're good friends, but they're very different.

Alex and Sam

Alex and Sam are good friends, but they're very different. Alex is tall and has blond hair and blue eyes. Sam is short and has black hair and brown eyes. Alex is thin; Sam is fat.

Sam and Alex also like to do different things. Sam likes to read, and he goes to the library a lot. Alex doesn't read much, and he never goes to the library. Sam likes Italian food and eats a lot. Alex likes French food, but he doesn't eat much. Sam is a great cook. Alex never cooks. Sam and Alex are very different, but they're good friends.

WRITING A STORY

Write a story comparing Pam and Laura. They're good friends, but they're very different. You may get some ideas from the story about Alex and Sam, but write your own story.

Pam and Laura

Pam and Laura are good friends, but they're very different. Pam is _____

_____. Laura is _____

_____. Pam is _____

_____. Laura is _____

_____.

Pam and Laura also like to do different things. Pam likes to _____

_____. Laura likes to _____

_____. Pam _____

_____. Laura _____

_____.

Michelle Loves to Shop and Talk

Reread the story "Michelle Loves to Shop and Talk" (page 19 of **The Pizza Tastes Great**) before doing the Story Review, Word Review, and Word and Story Review.

STORY REVIEW

If the sentence is true, write **T**. If it's false, write **F** and change it to a true statement.

1. _____ Dave loves to spend money.
   _____

2. _____ Michelle likes to buy new clothes and things for the house.
   _____

3. _____ Dave doesn't like to fight with his wife.
   _____

4. _____ He talks a lot.
   _____

5. _____ Everyone knows what Michelle is thinking.
   _____

6. _____ Dave and Michelle like to watch sports on TV.
   _____

7. _____ When she's driving alone, she listens to the news.
   _____

WORD REVIEW

Complete the sentences with these words.

because	quiet	both	about

1. & 2. Why are you so _____?

What are you thinking _____?

3. Beth eats out a lot _____ she doesn't like to cook.

4. I'm going to buy _____ sweaters. They're nice.

friendly	same	fighting	very

5. Emma and Aaron work in the _____ office.

6. Cindy is _____. That's why everyone likes her.

7. The coffee is _____ hot.

8. Are the children _____ again?

WORD AND STORY REVIEW

Complete the dialog with these words and practice it with a partner.

alone	shopping	clothes	buy
listening	spend	few	save

A New Dress

Michelle is going shopping. She wants Dave to go with her, but he has a lot to do this morning.

Michelle: What are you doing, dear?

Dave: I'm _____ to the news.

Michelle: Do you want to go _____ with me?

Dave: When are you going?

Michelle: In a _____ minutes.

Dave: No, I have a lot to do this morning.

Michelle: OK. I can go _____.

Dave: What are you going to _____?

Michelle: A new dress and shoes.

Dave: You _____ a lot of money on _____.

Michelle: Well, I want to look nice.

Dave: That's good, but we want to _____ some money too.

Michelle: Honey, I need a new dress and shoes.

Dave: OK, OK, but don't spend too much.

MATCHING

Match the words in Column A with their definitions or descriptions in Column B. Print the letters on the blank lines.

	Column A		Column B
_____	**1.** relax	**A.**	weighing a lot
_____	**2.** both	**B.**	what I like the most
_____	**3.** key	**C.**	to keep
_____	**4.** save	**D.**	having a lot to do
_____	**5.** heavy	**E.**	and no more
_____	**6.** menu	**F.**	to rest
_____	**7.** favorite	**G.**	it locks doors
_____	**8.** never	**H.**	a list of food and prices
_____	**9.** busy	**I.**	the two of them
10. only		**J.**	at no time

ABOUT ME

Complete these sentences.

1. I like to buy _____.

2. I like to listen to _____.

3. I like to save _____.

4. Sometimes I fight with _____.

5. I often think about _____.

6. I like to talk about _____.

7. Sometimes I'm late for _____.

8. I'm very _____.

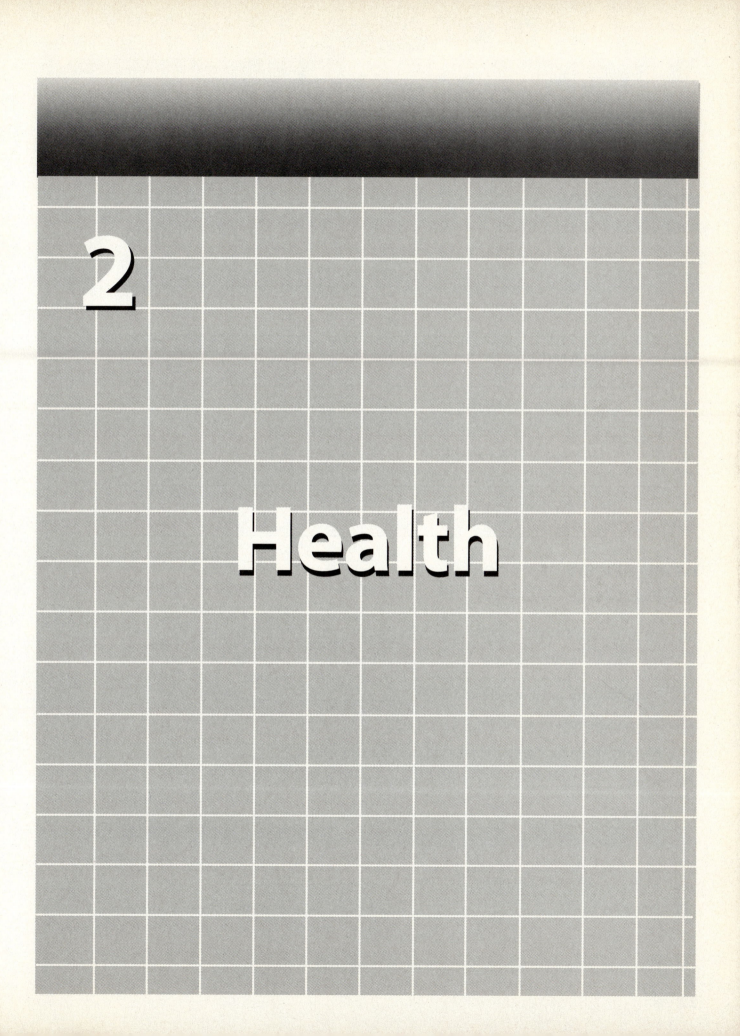

2

Health

A Toothache

Reread the dialog "A Toothache" (page 25 of **The Pizza Tastes Great**) before doing the dialog and word reviews.

DIALOG REVIEW

If the sentence is true, write **T**. *If it's false, write* **F** *and change it to a true statement.*

1. _____ Chen asks what time it is.

   _____

2. _____ It's ten o'clock in the morning.

   _____

3. _____ Chen is early.

   _____

4. _____ He's going to the dentist.

   _____

5. _____ Lin is going to drive him there.

   _____

6. _____ Chen's toothache isn't bad.

   _____

WORD REVIEW

Complete the sentences with these words.

there	sure	time	o'clock

1. "Can you help me move this table?" "_____, that's easy."

2. The game starts at eight _____.

3. It's only three blocks to the post office. You can walk _____.

4. What _____ do you want to go to the movies?

drive	sorry	toothache	hear

5. Gino isn't going to the dance. He has a _____.

6. I'm going to _____ to the park. Do you want to come?

7. Can you _____ me?

8. I'm _____ that we can't help you.

22

A HEADACHE

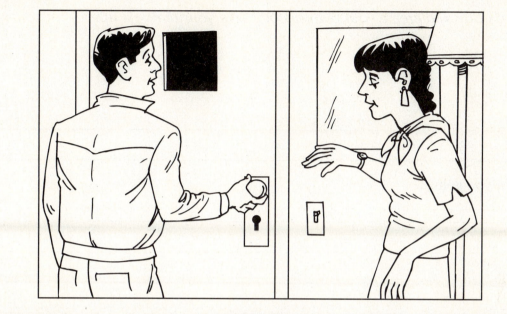

WORD BANK

Glad means happy.
A **headache** is a pain in your head. (*headache = head + ache*)

Complete the dialog with these words and practice it with a partner.

too	early	with	glad	party	headache

Mike is talking to his sister, Lauren. He's going to a party.

Mike: What time is it?

Lauren: Seven-thirty.

Mike: Good. I'm _____.

Lauren: Where are you going?

Mike: To a _____.

Lauren: Is your wife going _____ you?

Mike: No, she has a _____.

Lauren: Is it bad?

Mike: Not _____ bad.

Lauren: I'm _____ to hear that.

WRITING A DIALOG

Work with a partner and create your own dialog. Give your dialog a title.

_____

A: What time is it?

B: _____

A: _____

B: Where are you going?

A: _____

B: _____

A: _____

B: _____

ACHES

Circle how often you have these problems.

1. **headache**   frequently   sometimes   almost never   never

2. **toothache**   frequently   sometimes   almost never   never

3. **stomachache**   frequently   sometimes   almost never   never

4. **earache**   frequently   sometimes   almost never   never

5. **I get sick.**   frequently   sometimes   almost never   never

Sneezing a Lot

Reread the dialog "Sneezing a Lot" (page 28 of **The Pizza Tastes Great**) before doing the dialog and word reviews.

DIALOG REVIEW

If the sentence is true, write **T**. If it's false, write **F** and change it to a true statement.

1. _____ Nicole says she has a headache.

_____

2. _____ She has a cold.

_____

3. _____ She's not sneezing much.

_____

4. _____ Kevin hopes Nicole feels better.

_____

5. _____ She's taking cold medicine.

_____

6. _____ It keeps her awake.

_____

WORD REVIEW

Complete the sentences with these words.

soon	feel	sneezes	sleepy

1. I _____ great. And you?

2. The bus will be here _____.

3. I'm tired and _____. It's late.

4. When someone _____, I say "God bless you."

hope	cold	every	better

5. I think I'm getting a _____.

6. Marissa was very sick, but she's _____ now.

7. I _____ you like my idea.

8. Ahmad buys the newspaper _____ morning.

DO YOU FEEL HOT?

WORD BANK

Bit means a small amount.
The normal **temperature** of our body is 98.6° Fahrenheit.

Complete the dialog with these words and practice it with a partner.

temperature	today	bit	sick	medicine	why

Ryan is sick. He's not going to work today. He's talking to his mother.

Ryan: I can't go to work _____.

Audrey: _____ not?

Ryan: I'm _____.

Audrey: Do you feel hot?

Ryan: Very. My _____ is 102.

Audrey: Are you taking any _____?

Ryan: Aspirin.

Audrey: Is it helping?

Ryan: A little _____.

Audrey: I hope you feel better.

Ryan: Thank you.

INTERVIEWING

Ask a partner these questions.

1. May I ask you some questions?
2. How do you feel?
3. When you get a headache, do you take anything for it?
4. What do you take? Does it help much?
5. Can you drive?
6. Do you have a driver's license?
7. Do you like parties? A lot?
8. Do you go to many parties?

ABOUT ME

Complete these sentences.

1. I'm glad that _____.
2. I'm sorry that _____.
3. I hope that _____.
4. I'm sure that _____ soon.
5. I'm going to _____.
6. I _____ everyday.

I Don't Feel Well

Reread the dialog "I Don't Feel Well" (page 31 of **The Pizza Tastes Great**) before doing the dialog and word reviews.

DIALOG REVIEW

If the sentence is true, write **T**. If it's false, write **F** and change it to a true statement.

1. _____ Anish is looking for his jacket.

   _____

2. _____ He feels OK.

   _____

3. _____ He has a fever.

   _____

4. _____ He has a pain in his chest.

   _____

5. _____ He has an appointment at one-thirty.

   _____

6. _____ Anish will see Risha later.

   _____

WORD REVIEW

Complete the sentences with these words.

looking for	pain	appointment	well

1. Dennis has a _____ in his side.

2. I'm _____ my watch. Did you see it?

3. Rita isn't going to school today. She's not _____.

4. Julio has a three o'clock _____ with a lawyer.

good-bye	serious	fever	later

5. The baby feels warm. I think he has a _____.

6. I'm leaving. _____.

7. Donna isn't here now. She's coming _____.

8. John is sick, but it's not _____.

28

A PAIN IN THE SHOULDER

WORD BANK

The **shoulder** is the part of the body between the neck and the arm.
You say **too bad** to show that you're sorry about something.

Complete the dialog with these words and practice it with a partner.

think	**keys**	**shoulder**	**table**	**something**	**sleep**

Jack is talking to his sister, Beth. She is looking for her car keys. She is going to the doctor.

Jack: Are you looking for _____?

Beth: Yes, my car _____.

Jack: They're on the dining room _____.

Beth: Thanks. I'm going to the doctor.

Jack: I hope it's not serious.

Beth: I don't _____ it is, but I'm not sure.

Jack: What's the problem?

Beth: I have a pain in my _____.

Jack: Is it bad?

Beth: Very. I can't _____ at night.

Jack: That's too bad.

WRITING A DIALOG

Work with a partner and create your own dialog. Give your dialog a title.

_____

A: Are you looking for something?

B: Yes, my _____ .

A: They're (It's) _____ .

B: Thanks. _____

A: _____

B: _____

A: _____

B: _____

SIMON SAYS, "TOUCH YOUR . . ."

Work in pairs. One student says, "Touch your nose." The other student touches his or her nose. The student continues reading from the list, but doesn't read in order. In numbers 4, 7, and 20, the student says, "Point to your . . ."

1. head
2. hair
3. nose
4. eye   (point to)
5. ear
6. lip
7. teeth   (point to)
8. neck
9. shoulder
10. arm

11. elbow
12. hand
13. finger
14. chest
15. stomach
16. back
17. leg
18. knee
19. ankle
20. toe   (point to)

A Sore Throat

Reread the dialog "A Sore Throat" (page 34 of **The Pizza Tastes Great**) before doing the dialog and word reviews.

DIALOG REVIEW

If the sentence is true, write **T**. If it's false, write **F** and change it to a true statement.

1. _____ Kathy sounds terrible.
   _____

2. _____ She has a sore leg.
   _____

3. _____ It hurts when she walks.
   _____

4. _____ She's taking hot tea and honey.
   _____

5. _____ She's going to work today.
   _____

6. _____ She thinks she'll feel better tomorrow.
   _____

WORD REVIEW

Complete the sentences with these words.

voice	sounds	sore	terrible

1. I'll never go to that restaurant again. The food was _____.

2. Your stereo _____ great.

3. I have a _____ back. I'm resting it.

4. The dog knows my _____. He comes when I call him.

stay	so	should	hurts

5. I'm very tired. I _____ get more sleep.

6. _____ with us! Don't go!

7. My knee _____ when I walk.

8. Who says Victor isn't a good cook? His wife says _____.

THE FLU

WORD BANK
The **flu** is like a bad cold, but it's more serious.
What's wrong means what's the problem.

Complete the dialog with these words and practice it with a partner.

should	idea	feel	help	flu	taking

Nadia doesn't feel well. She thinks she has the flu. She's talking to her friend Yuri.

Nadia: I _____ terrible.

 Yuri: What's wrong?

Nadia: I think I have the _____.

 Yuri: You _____ be in bed.

Nadia: I know. I have a fever.

 Yuri: Are you _____ any medicine?

Nadia: No. I want to call the doctor first.

 Yuri: That's a good _____.

Nadia: I'm resting and drinking more water.

 Yuri: That should _____.

INTERVIEWING

Ask a partner these questions.

1. May I ask you some questions?
2. Do you stay home from work (or school) a lot because you're sick?
3. Do you go to a doctor much?
4. What do you think of your doctor? Is he or she excellent, very good, good, or OK?
5. What do you do if you have a fever of 100°?
6. What do you do if you have a fever of 103°?
7. Did you ever have the flu? Was it bad?
8. Do you think it's a bad idea to go to work (or school) if you have the flu? Why?

ABOUT ME

Complete these sentences.

1. I think it's a **good idea** for me to _____.
2. I don't think that _____, but I'm **not sure**.
3. **Tomorrow** I'm going to _____.
4. Sometimes my _____ **hurts**.
5. I know **I should** _____.
6. When I **stay home** from school (work), I _____
_____.

A Doctor

Reread the story "A Doctor" (page 37 of **The Pizza Tastes Great**) before doing the Story Review, Word Review, and Word and Story Review.

STORY REVIEW

*If the sentence is true, write **T**. If it's false, write **F** and change it to a true statement.*

1. ____ Carmen is studying to be a lawyer.
   _____

2. ____ She's very smart.
   _____

3. ____ Her boyfriend fixes computers.
   _____

4. ____ Her parents are from Mexico.
   _____

5. ____ They're helping to pay her bills for medical school.
   _____

6. ____ Carmen's father works in a store.
   _____

7. ____ Carmen has a brother, but no sisters.
   _____

WORD REVIEW

Complete the sentences with these words.

find time	another	go out	marry

1. We need _____ chair.

2. Derek loves Sally, and he wants to _____ her.

3. It's not easy to _____ to read.

4. It's very cold. I don't want to _____ .

hard	have to	finish	department store

5. We're going to play cards when we _____ dinner.

6. These math problems are _____.

7. Yoshi and Peggy like to shop in _____.

8. I _____ go to school.

WORD AND STORY REVIEW

Complete the dialog with these words and practice it with a partner.

expensive	repairs	a lot	single
graduate	bills	last	smart

How's Carmen Doing?

Jackie is talking to Carlos, Carmen's father. Jackie is a friend of the family.

Jackie: How's Carmen doing?

Carlos: Fine. She's studying to be a doctor.

Jackie: That's great! She's very _____.

Carlos: Yes, and she studies _____.

Jackie: When is she going to _____?

Carlos: In June. This is her _____ year.

Jackie: Is medical school very _____?

Carlos: Yes. And we're helping to pay her _____.

Jackie: Is Carmen married?

Carlos: No, she's _____, but she has a boyfriend.

Jackie: What does he do?

Carlos: He _____ computers.

Jackie: Does he make a lot of money?

Carlos: I think so.

READING AN AUTOBIOGRAPHY

Read the story about Gloria, a college student.

Gloria

My name is Gloria, and I'm 20. I'm from Bogotá, Colombia. I speak Spanish, and I'm learning English. I go to Passaic County Community College in Paterson, New Jersey. I live in Paterson with my dad and younger brother. My mom and my sister, who is ten, live in Bogotá. They're going to come to the United States next year. I will be so happy to see them again.

I'm studying to be a computer programmer. It's not easy, but that's what I want to be. Most of my classes are in the morning. I study in the afternoon, and I work as a waitress at night. It's not a great job, but I need the money. I think I'm lucky. I have a lot of friends, and I like school. In a few years, I will have a good job.

WRITING AN AUTOBIOGRAPHY

Write two paragraphs about yourself. You can get some ideas from the autobiography of Gloria, but write your own story. You can use your name for the title.

_____

My name is _____, and I'm from _____

_____

_____

_____

_____

_____

_____

_____

_____

_____

_____

_____

_____

She Wants to Be Herself

Reread the story "She Wants to Be Herself" (page 41 of **The Pizza Tastes Great**) before doing the Story Review, Word Review, and Word and Story Review.

STORY REVIEW

If the sentence is true, write **T**. If it's false, write **F** and change it to a true statement.

1. _____ Regina talks a lot.

_____

2. _____ She wants to be like her sister.

_____

3. _____ She goes for long rides on her bike.

_____

4. _____ She collects stamps.

_____

5. _____ She wants to be a Spanish teacher.

_____

6. _____ Some of her friends say teachers don't make a lot of money.

_____

7. _____ She thinks money is the most important thing in life.

_____

WORD REVIEW

Complete the sentences with these words.

know about	member	belongs	first

1. Doug _____ to a computer club.

2. Does your father _____ the accident?

3. Our _____ class is at nine o'clock.

4. Jane is a _____ of the volleyball team.

born	than	language	well

5. Alaska is larger _____ California.

6. Vanessa is a good swimmer. She swims _____.

7. Abraham Lincoln was _____ in Kentucky on February 12, 1809.

8. I think everyone should learn a second _____.

WORD AND STORY REVIEW

Complete the dialog with these words and practice it with a partner.

rides	junior	hobby	herself
compare	collects	annoys	still

Stamps for Regina

Jackie is talking to Carlos, Regina and Carmen's father. Jackie is a friend of the family.

Jackie: How's Regina doing?

Carlos: She's doing well. She's a _____ in high school.

Jackie: Does she _____ look like her sister?

Carlos: Yes, but I never _____ her to Carmen.

Jackie: Why not?

Carlos: It _____ her.

Jackie: I didn't know that.

Carlos: Yes, she wants to be _____.

Jackie: Does she still go for long bike _____?

Carlos: Yes, she does.

Jackie: I have some stamps for her.

Carlos: Thank you. That's nice of you.

Jackie: I know she _____ them.

Carlos: Yes, it's her favorite _____.

Jackie: That's great.

READING A STORY

Read the story about Rajesh Patel, a high-school teacher.

A Good Friend

I want to tell you a little about my good friend Rajesh Patel. He's from India. His first language is Gujarati, but he speaks English very well. He teaches math and computer science in a large high school in Boston. His students like him because he's friendly. They also learn a lot in his class.

Rajesh loves music and sports. He plays the piano well and likes to listen to all kinds of music. Baseball is his favorite sport and mine too. Sometimes we go to watch the Boston Red Sox play.

When I have a problem, I always talk to Rajesh. He listens very carefully, and we discuss the situation. When he has a problem, he comes to me. I listen to him and tell him what I think. He's my best friend.

WRITING A STORY

Write two or three paragraphs about a good friend. You may get some ideas from the story "A Good Friend," but write your own story and give it a title.

MATCHING

Match the words in Column A with their definitions or descriptions in Column B. Print the letters on the blank lines.

	Column A	Column B
_____	1. expensive	A. happy
_____	2. cold (noun)	B. one more
_____	3. almost	C. continuing to
_____	4. glad	D. it makes us cough
_____	5. bills	E. to be a member
_____	6. still	F. a little less than
_____	7. bit	G. after all the others
_____	8. belong	H. costing a lot
_____	9. last	I. a small amount
_____	10. another	J. we have to pay them

3

Birthdays

Reread the dialog "Good News" (page 47 of **The Pizza Tastes Great**) before doing the dialog and word reviews.

DIALOG REVIEW

If the sentence is true, write **T**. *If it's false, write* **F** *and change it to a true statement.*

1. _____ Andy has bad news.
   _____

2. _____ Kim is going to have a baby.
   _____

3. _____ Andy and Laura are very happy.
   _____

4. _____ Kim wants a boy.
   _____

5. _____ The baby is due at the end of December.
   _____

6. _____ Laura is going to phone Kim.
   _____

WORD REVIEW

Complete the sentences with these words.

so	news	phone	great

1. I should _____ my sister.

2. & 3. It's _____ hot today.

   It's a _____ day to go swimming.

4. Everyone knows about the fire. That's old _____ .

due	or	me too	beginning

5. Do you live in a house _____ an apartment?

6. The _____ of the show was great.

7. The telephone bill is _____ today.

8. Greg likes to play basketball. _____ . It's my favorite sport.

A BETTER JOB

WORD BANK

To **begin** is to start.
Better (than) is the comparative of *good*.

Complete the dialog with these words and practice it with a partner.

| post office | job | hear | begin | tell | better |

Brenda and Austin are friends. Brenda has good news for Austin.

Brenda: I have something to _____ you.

Austin: What is it?

Brenda: I have a new _____.

Austin: Is it _____ than the one you have?

Brenda: Much.

Austin: That's good news.

Brenda: I _____ tomorrow.

Austin: Where are you going to work?

Brenda: In the _____.

Austin: Will you make more money?

Brenda: A lot more.

Austin: I'm glad to _____ that.

WRITING A DIALOG

Work with a partner and create your own dialog. Give your dialog a title.

_____

A: I have something to tell you.

B: What is it?

A: I _____.

B: _____

A: _____

B: _____

A: _____

B: _____

GOOD AND BAD NEWS

Give three examples of good news.

1. _____

2. _____

3. _____

Give three examples of bad news.

1. _____

2. _____

3. _____

MONTHS OF THE YEAR

December is the last month of the year. Write the first 11 months on the lines below.

1. _____   5. _____   9. _____

2. _____   6. _____   10. _____

3. _____   7. _____   11. _____

4. _____   8. _____   12. *December*

That's Too Bad!

Reread the dialog "That's Too Bad!," (page 50 of **The Pizza Tastes Great**) before doing the dialog and word reviews.

DIALOG REVIEW

*If the sentence is true, write **T**. If it's false, write **F** and change it to a true statement.*

1. _____ Today is Maria's birthday.
   _____

2. _____ Maria is Luz's sister.
   _____

3. _____ Luz is going to Maria's house after dinner.
   _____

4. _____ Maria is 30 years old.
   _____

5. _____ She's pretty and she's nice.
   _____

6. _____ Ramon is happy that she's married.
   _____

WORD REVIEW

Complete the sentences with these words.

too	cousin	birthday	age

1. My _____ is July 9.

2. Alan plays the piano, and I do _____.

3. Doris doesn't want anyone to know her _____.

4. Heather isn't my sister. She's my _____.

too bad	married	how	pretty

5. I like your yard. It's very _____.

6. Eileen is _____. That's her husband.

7. _____ tall is your brother?

8. It's _____ you can't go to the game tonight.

IS HE MARRIED?

WORD BANK
Handsome means good-looking. Handsome is usually said of a man. To **meet** is to see and talk to someone for the first time.

Complete the dialog with these words and practice it with a partner.

handsome	older	meet	so	tonight	sure

Amy is talking to Tom. His brother, Ed, is 26 today. Amy wants to meet him.

Tom: Today is my brother's birthday.

Amy: How old is he?

Tom: Ed's 26.

Amy: Hmm. He's a little _____ than I am.

Tom: We're having a party for him _____.

Amy: Is he married?

Tom: No, he's single.

Amy: Is he _____?

Tom: I think _____.

Amy: Can I go to the party?

Tom: _____. Why not?

Amy: Thanks. I have to _____ him.

WRITING A PARAGRAPH

Write one paragraph of about six or seven sentences describing the perfect girlfriend or boyfriend, or the perfect husband or wife. For example, "Donna is a perfect girlfriend. She . . ." "Jack is a perfect husband. He . . ."

_____

_____

_____

_____

_____

_____

_____

HOW IMPORTANT IS IT?

Circle the number that tells how important these qualities are in a husband or wife.

| 1 = not important |
| 2 = not that important |
| 3 = important |
| 4 = very important |
| 5 = very, very important |

A.	is handsome or pretty	1	2	3	4	5
B.	loves you a lot	1	2	3	4	5
C.	understands you	1	2	3	4	5
D.	has a lot of money	1	2	3	4	5
E.	is intelligent	1	2	3	4	5
F.	has a good education	1	2	3	4	5
G.	likes what you like	1	2	3	4	5
H.	is your age or close to it	1	2	3	4	5

A Cake

Reread the dialog "A Cake" (page 53 of **The Pizza Tastes Great**) before doing the dialog and word reviews.

DIALOG REVIEW

*If the sentence is true, write **T**. If it's false, write **F** and change it to a true statement.*

1. _____ There are no bakeries near Erin's house.

   _____

2. _____ Scott wants to buy a birthday cake.

   _____

3. _____ It's his wife's birthday.

   _____

4. _____ He's going to get some bread for Erin.

   _____

5. _____ He's also getting some cookies for her.

   _____

6. _____ She's going to pay Scott when he gets back.

   _____

WORD REVIEW

Complete the sentences with these words.

near	is there	get back	anything

1. _____ a doctor on the plane?

2. Mr. Rockefeller can buy _____ he wants. He's rich.

3. Sit _____ the door.

4. Did Kristina _____ from the store?

pay	bakery	else	get

5. I'm going to my favorite _____ to get some donuts.

6. You can _____ by check.

7. What time do you _____ to school?

8. Who _____ is on the team?

GO IMMEDIATELY

WORD BANK

Immediately means now.
Ready means prepared to act.

Complete the dialog with these words and practice it with a partner.

ready	drive	terrible	hospital	should	pain

Brandon is visiting his cousin Ashley. He wants to go to the hospital. Ashley takes him there.

Brandon: Is there a _____ near here?

Ashley: Yes. I can _____ you there in two minutes.

Brandon: Thanks.

Ashley: What's the problem?

Brandon: I have a _____ in my chest and arms.

Ashley: Is it bad?

Brandon: It's _____ .

Ashley: We _____ go immediately.

Brandon: I'm _____ .

Ashley: Good. I'll get my car.

Brandon: I hope it's not my heart.

WRITING A DIALOG

Work with a partner and create your own dialog. Give your dialog a title.

_____

A: Is there a _____ near here?

B: Yes, I can drive you there in two minutes.

A: Thanks.

B: _____

A: _____

B: _____

A: _____

B: _____

WHY ARE YOU GOING TO THESE PLACES?

Think of why you go to these places and complete the sentences.

1. I'm going to the supermarket to _____.

2. I'm going to the library to _____.

3. I'm going to the bank to _____.

4. I'm going to the pharmacy to _____.

5. I'm going to the park to _____.

6. I'm going to McDonald's to _____.

7. I'm going to the laundromat to _____.

8. I'm going to my friend's house to _____.

A Birthday Present

Reread the dialog "A Birthday Present" (page 56 of **The Pizza Tastes Great**) before doing the dialog and word reviews.

DIALOG REVIEW

If the sentence is true, write **T**. If it's false, write **F** and change it to a true statement.

1. _____ Erica is going to get Reggie a shirt for his birthday.
   _____

2. _____ She got him a sweater last year.
   _____

3. _____ She wants to get him something different this year.
   _____

4. _____ Nick asks about getting him a briefcase.
   _____

5. _____ Erica doesn't like that idea.
   _____

6. _____ Reggie won't use the briefcase much.
   _____

WORD REVIEW

Complete the sentences with these words.

of course	briefcase	yet	got

1. My husband isn't home _____.
2. Our teacher usually leaves his _____ on his desk.
3. Larry _____ his son a bicycle for Christmas.
4. _____ we'll help you.

how about	let	different	one

5. _____ me take your coat.
6. This store doesn't have what I want. I'm going to another _____.
7. _____ chicken soup for lunch?
8. We're moving our money to a _____ bank.

MARRIED TWENTY-FIVE YEARS

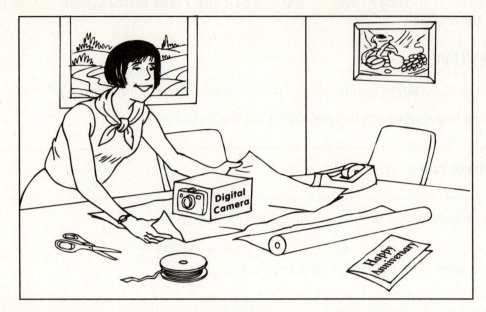

WORD BANK

An **anniversary** is the date on which something special happened.
A **picture** is a photo.
Special means very important, not usual.

Complete the dialog with these words and practice it with a partner.

> expensive   a lot   send   how long   anniversary   camera

Megan and Joe are talking about what to get their friends Bill and Sue for their wedding anniversary.

Megan: What can we get Bill and Sue for their _____?

Joe: I don't know. Let me think.

Megan: We can _____ them flowers.

Joe: No, I don't want to do that.

Megan: How about a _____?

Joe: That'll be _____.

Megan: I know, but it's a special anniversary.

Joe: _____ will they be married?

Megan: Twenty-five years.

Joe: Wow! That *is* special! Get the camera.

Megan: They'll use it _____.

Joe: Of course. They like to take pictures.

INTERVIEWING

Ask a partner these questions.

1. May I ask you some questions?

2. When do people give presents?

3. Why do people give presents?

4. Name some presents that people often give.

5. Do you have a briefcase? Do you use it much?

6. Do you like to take pictures?

7. Do you take many?

8. When do people take pictures?

SENTENCE COMPLETION

Complete these sentences.

1. I want to **get** a new _____.

2. I didn't _____ **yet**.

3. **Let** me _____.

4. **How about** _____?

5. My _____ is (are) **getting old**.

6. My _____ is (are) in my **briefcase**.

7. I _____ **every day**.

8. **Of course** I _____.

ABOUT YOU

Answer these questions with **Of course** *or* **Of course not**; *or* **Yes, I do** *or* **No, I don't**.

1. Do you want to be rich? _____.

2. Do you like to get up early? _____.

3. Do you like ice cream? _____.

4. Do you want to learn English? _____.

5. Do you speak Spanish? _____.

6. Do you like the summer? _____.

7. Do you watch TV at night? _____.

Forty and Getting Gray

Reread the story "Forty and Getting Gray" (page 59 of **The Pizza Tastes Great**) before doing the Story Review, Word Review, and Word and Story Review.

STORY REVIEW

If the sentence is true, write **T**. *If it's false, write* **F** *and change it to a true statement.*

1. _____ Jim is relaxing and watching a movie.
   _____

2. _____ He doesn't like his job.
   _____

3. _____ Last year he saved a woman's life.
   _____

4. _____ He had a birthday last week.
   _____

5. _____ His hair is getting gray, and he feels old.
   _____

6. _____ Sara is sitting on the sofa and reading a book.
   _____

7. _____ She works for a large insurance company.
   _____

WORD REVIEW

Complete the sentences with these words.

every	on fire	strong	relax

1. Take a 20-minute break and _____.

2. Oh no! Our house is _____!

3. Marina goes for a walk _____ afternoon.

4. You're _____. Help me carry these packages to the car, please.

feel	pay attention	brave	last

5. _____ to what you're doing.

6. Our _____ math test was long.

7. I don't _____ great, but I'm going to work.

8. The soldiers are fighting hard to save the city. They're _____.

WORD AND STORY REVIEW

Complete the dialog with these words and practice it with a partner.

jog	computers	getting	insurance
well	saved	interesting	still

A Firefighter

Linda meets Jim at a party. They're talking about Jim and his wife, Sara.

Linda: What's your job?

Jim: I'm a firefighter.

Linda: Do you like your work?

Jim: I love it. Last year I _____ a woman's life.

Linda: That's great!

Jim: And today's my birthday.

Linda: Happy birthday!

Jim: Thank you. I'm 40, and my hair is _____ gray.

Linda: But you _____ look young.

Jim: Well, I play tennis every week, and I _____ a lot.

Linda: Are you married?

Jim: Yes. My wife works for a large _____ company.

Linda: That must be _____.

Jim: It is. She works with _____.

Linda: Does she like her job?

Jim: Yes, and it pays _____.

Linda: That's good.

READING A STORY

Read the story about Dick and Nancy. He's an engineer and she's a teacher.

An Engineer and a Teacher

It's nine o'clock at night, and Dick is watching a football game on TV. He loves football and watches it every Monday night during the football season. Dick is 74 and he's an engineer, but he doesn't work anymore. That's why he spends a lot of time watching TV, especially football games and old movies.

Dick's wife, Nancy, is sitting at the dining room table. She doesn't like football and never watches it on TV. Nancy is a high-school English teacher, and she's correcting tests. Tomorrow is her birthday. She's going to be 65, and her health is excellent. She never thinks of herself as old, but most of her students do. Of course they're only 15 or 16, and they think a person is old at 40.

WRITING A STORY

Write two paragraphs about a married couple. In the first paragraph, write about the husband. In the second paragraph, write about the wife. You may get some ideas from the story "An Engineer and a Teacher," but write your own story and give it a title.

_____

_____

_____

_____

_____

_____

_____

_____

_____

_____

On the Phone Too Much

*Reread the story "On the Phone Too Much" (page 63 of **The Pizza Tastes Great**) before doing the Story Review, Word Review, and Word and Story Review.*

STORY REVIEW

*If the sentence is true, write **T**. If it's false, write **F** and change it to a true statement.*

1. _____ Dianne is 12 and in the seventh grade.
   _____

2. _____ She talks a lot on the phone.
   _____

3. _____ Jim or Sara usually answers the phone.
   _____

4. _____ History and English are Dianne's favorite subjects.
   _____

5. _____ Dianne wants to study to be a chemist.
   _____

6. _____ Frank likes to study.
   _____

7. _____ His big interests are basketball, music, and his girlfriend.
   _____

WORD REVIEW

Complete the sentences with these words.

change	too	main	probably

1. It'll _____ rain tomorrow.
2. Courtney wants to _____ jobs. She doesn't like what she's doing.
3. The _____ post office is five blocks from here.
4. I'm _____ tired to drive.

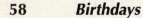

passed	hope	inches	ringing

5. I _____ Jonathan can come with us.

6. The alarm clock is _____. It's time to get up.

7. Michelle thinks she _____ the chemistry test.

8. John is five feet ten _____ tall.

WORD AND STORY REVIEW

Complete the dialog with these words and practice it with a partner.

best	usually	second	interests
change	hard	all right	favorites

High School Students

Ann is visiting her friends Jim and Sara. She is asking Jim about their children.

Ann: How are Dianne and Frank?

Jim: Fine. Dianne is in her _____ year of high school.

Ann: Does she like school?

Jim: Yes, and she studies _____.

Ann: What subjects does she like?

Jim: Math and science are her _____.

Ann: Does she do well in them?

Jim: Yes, but we're having a problem. She's on the phone too much.

Ann: High school students _____ are.

Jim: I know, but we want her to _____.

Ann: How's Frank doing in school?

Jim: _____, but he doesn't like to study.

Ann: What does he like to do?

Jim: His big _____ are basketball, music, and girls.

Ann: Is he a good basketball player?

Jim: He's the _____ player on the team.

Ann: That's wonderful!

MATCHING

Match the words in Column A with their definitions or descriptions in Column B. Print the letters on the blank lines.

	Column A	Column B
_____	1. subjects	A. to give money to
_____	2. get back	B. most important
_____	3. cousin	C. math, science, history
_____	4. inches	D. to run
_____	5. pay	E. we use it to carry important papers
_____	6. bakery	F. to return
_____	7. usually	G. there are 12 in a foot
_____	8. jog	H. it sells cakes, cookies, and bread
_____	9. main	I. a relative
_____	10. briefcase	J. most of the time

ABOUT ME

Complete these sentences by writing **never**, **sometimes**, **often**, **usually**, *or* **always** *in the blank spaces.*

1. I _____ read the newspaper in the morning.

2. I _____ drink juice for breakfast.

3. I _____ chew gum.

4. I _____ listen to music.

5. I _____ go to the movies.

6. I _____ play cards.

7. I _____ watch the news on TV.

8. I _____ study at night.

4

Cars
and Planes

Washing the Car

Reread the dialog "Washing the Car" (page 69 of **The Pizza Tastes Great**) before doing the dialog and word reviews.

DIALOG REVIEW

If the sentence is true, write **T**. *If it's false, write* **F** *and change it to a true statement.*

1. _____ Dan's in front of his house.

   _____

2. _____ He's fixing his car.

   _____

3. _____ His car is usually dirty.

   _____

4. _____ He takes good care of his car.

   _____

5. _____ He cleans his room a lot.

   _____

6. _____ His room is a mess.

   _____

WORD REVIEW

Complete the sentences with these words.

mess	always	in front of	in order

1. There's an American flag _____ our school.
2. It was a big party, and our kitchen is a _____.
3. This room looks great. Everything is _____.
4. I _____ go to the bank on Friday afternoon.

right	dirty	nothing	takes care of

5. These clothes are _____. I'm going to wash them.
6. Who _____ the baby when you're at work?
7. The doctor says I'll be fine. I hope he's _____.
8. If you want that box, take it. There's _____ in it.

THAT'S WHAT HIS WIFE SAYS

WORD BANK

Across means on the other side of.
Right means OK or what should be.

Complete the dialog with these words and practice it with a partner.

nice	right	helping	tell	paint	across

Amanda and Jacob are visiting their cousin Oscar for a few days. Amanda asks Jacob where Oscar is.

Amanda: Where's Oscar?

Jacob: He's _____ the street.

Amanda: What's he doing?

Jacob: He's _____ his friend.

Amanda: To do what?

Jacob: To _____ his house.

Amanda: That's _____ of Oscar.

Jacob: Yes, but don't _____ his wife.

Amanda: Why not?

Jacob: He never does anything at home.

Amanda: That's not _____.

Jacob: That's what his wife says.

WRITING A DIALOG

Work with a partner and create your own dialog. Give your dialog a title.

_____

A: Where's _____?

B: He's (She's) across the street.

A: What's he (she) doing?

B: _____

A: _____

B: _____

A: _____

B: _____

ABOUT ME

*Complete these sentences by writing **never**, **sometimes**, **often**, **usually**, or **always** in the blank spaces.*

1. I _____ clean my room.

2. I _____ keep things in order.

3. I _____ take good care of my clothes.

4. I _____ wash the dishes.

5. I _____ wash my clothes.

6. I _____ help keep the house clean.

7. I _____ brush my teeth after breakfast.

8. I _____ wash my hair at night.

A Flat

Reread the dialog "A Flat" (page 72 of **The Pizza Tastes Great**) before doing the dialog and word reviews.

DIALOG REVIEW

If the sentence is true, write **T**. If it's false, write **F** and change it to a true statement.

1. _____ Alex's car is OK.

   _____

2. _____ Lauren checks the tires on his car.

   _____

3. _____ One of the front tires is flat.

   _____

4. _____ Alex doesn't know how to change a flat.

   _____

5. _____ Lauren changes the flat.

   _____

6. _____ Alex calls AAA on Lauren's cell.

   _____

WORD REVIEW

Complete the sentences with these words.

checks	darn it	flat	may

1. The mechanic at the gas station changed my _____ in ten minutes.

2. Kyle _____ his e-mail when he gets home from work.

3. We _____ get a new computer.

4. _____! I cut my finger.

me neither	pulled over	tires	wrong

5. What's _____ with this camera?

6. "I don't want to go to school today." "_____, but we have to."

7. We'll need new _____ soon.

8. The bus _____ and stopped to pick up a passenger.

I CAN'T GET INTO MY HOUSE

WORD BANK
To **climb** is to go up. To **fall** is to go down. **High** means a long distance from the ground. *Low* is the opposite of *high*. You use a **ladder** to climb up.

Complete the dialog with these words and practice it with a partner.

climbing	fall	wrong	high	maybe	garage

Dawn can't get into her house. Ted offers to help.

Ted: Is something _____?

Dawn: I can't get into my house.

Ted: _____ I can help.

Dawn: How?

Ted: By _____ in a window.

Dawn: But the windows are _____.

Ted: Do you have a ladder?

Dawn: Yes, there's one in the _____.

Ted: Good. Get it for me, please.

Dawn: Here's the ladder. Be careful!

Ted: Don't worry. I won't _____.

INTERVIEWING

Ask a partner these questions.

1. May I ask you some questions?

2. Are you careful to lock your house or apartment when you go out?

3. Did you ever lock your house and then not have the key to get in?

4. Do you think it's a good idea to leave an extra key somewhere, or with someone, in case you don't have your key?

5. Is it difficult to change a flat?

6. Do you know how to change a flat?

7. Do you think it's dangerous to talk on a cell phone when you're driving?

8. Why is it good to have a cell phone in a car?

SENTENCE COMPLETION

Complete these sentences.

1. The _____ is (are) **dirty**. I'm going to _____.

2. I have to **take care of** _____.

3. _____ is a **mess**.

4. **Darn it!** I _____.

5. I **may** _____ tomorrow.

6. It's **wrong** to _____.

7. "I don't like _____." "**Me neither.**"

A Car Loan

Reread the dialog "A Car Loan" (page 75 of **The Pizza Tastes Great**) before doing the dialog and word reviews.

DIALOG REVIEW

*If the sentence is true, write **T**. If it's false, write **F** and change it to a true statement.*

1. _____ Janet is going to take a bus to the bank.

   _____

2. _____ Tyrone has to cash a check.

   _____

3. _____ Janet needs a loan.

   _____

4. _____ She's going to buy a used car.

   _____

5. _____ Her car is five years old.

   _____

6. _____ New cars are expensive.

   _____

WORD REVIEW

Complete the sentences with these words.

apply	loan	wrong	costs

1. I don't need glasses. There's nothing _____ with my eyes.

2.–4. Kristin is going to _____ to college soon.

   It _____ a lot to go to college.

   Kristin is going to ask the bank for a _____.

about	cash	a lot of	have to

5. Where can I _____ this money order?

6. Alexi gets home from work _____ six o'clock.

7. I _____ wash my hands before we eat.

8. When it's hot, I drink _____ water.

BUYING A HOUSE

WORD BANK

To **be in trouble** means to have a problem.
Far means at a great distance.
A **kid** is a child. *Kid* is informal.

Complete the dialog with these words and practice it with a partner.

kids	trouble	close	far	lawyer	only

Asma and her husband are going to buy a house. She's talking to her brother Omar.

Omar: Where are you going?

Asma: I have to see a _____.

Omar: Are you in _____?

Asma: No, we're going to buy a house.

Omar: That's great! Is it _____ from here?

Asma: No, it's _____ four blocks away.

Omar: That's _____. I'm glad.

Asma: And it's only a block from the park.

Omar: That's nice for the _____.

Asma: That's right. They'll love it.

WRITING A DIALOG

Work with a partner and create your own dialog. Give your dialog a title.

_____

A: I'm going to buy a house.

B: That's great! Is it far from here?

A: _____.

B: _____.

A: _____.

B: _____.

A: _____.

B: _____.

SENTENCE COMPLETION

Complete these sentences.

1. Tomorrow I **have to** _____.

2. Something is **wrong** with my _____.

3. I want to **buy** a _____.

4. It'll **cost** about _____.

5. I have **a lot of** _____.

6. I don't have **a lot of** _____.

7. I live **close** to _____.

8. I live **far** from _____.

9. People **apply** for loans and jobs. People also **apply** for _____

_____.

Do You Like to Fly?

Reread the dialog "Do You Like to Fly?" (page 78 of **The Pizza Tastes Great**) before doing the dialog and word reviews.

DIALOG REVIEW

If the sentence is true, write **T**. If it's false, write **F** and change it to a true statement.

1. _____ Danielle is flying to Dallas, Texas.

   _____

2. _____ She's going there to visit a friend.

   _____

3. _____ Danielle and Justin like to fly.

   _____

4. _____ Danielle doesn't have to pay for her trip.

   _____

5. _____ She thinks it's foolish to be afraid to fly.

   _____

6. _____ She says almost everyone feels safe in a plane.

   _____

WORD REVIEW

Complete the sentences with these words.

understand	safe	maybe	meeting

1. Is it _____ to drink this water?

2. What time is our _____?

3. & 4. I don't _____ these math problems.

   _____ you can help me.

foolish	afraid	flying	trip

5. We had a great _____.

6. Some people are _____ to drive at night.

7. You're _____ to sit in the hot sun.

8. I'm _____ to San Francisco next week.

TO MEXICO

WORD BANK

Excited means very happy about something.
To **pack** is to put clothing and other things in a suitcase.
So means too or also.
A **vacation** is a time of rest from work or school.

Complete the dialog with these words and practice it with a partner.

excited	second	yet	trip	leaving	so

Vicky and her family are going to Mexico for their vacation. She is talking to Joshua; he works with her.

Joshua: Where are you going for your vacation?

Vicky: To Mexico.

Joshua: Is this your first time?

Vicky: No, it's our _____.

Joshua: When are you _____?

Vicky: Tomorrow morning at eight.

Joshua: Did you pack?

Vicky: Not _____.

Joshua: You must be _____ .

Vicky: Yes. And _____ are the kids.

Joshua: Have a nice _____ !

Vicky: Thanks. We will.

INTERVIEWING

Ask a partner these questions.

1. May I ask you some questions?

2. Do you like to fly?

3. Do you think it's safer to drive or to fly?

4. What do you know about Texas?

5. Where is Mexico?

6. Did you ever go to Mexico? If you did, why?

7. What language do most Mexicans speak?

8. Do you usually stay home for your vacation? If not, where do you go?

SENTENCE COMPLETION

Complete these sentences.

1. I don't **understand** _____ .

2. I think it's **foolish** to _____ .

3. It's **safe** to _____ .

4. It's not **safe** to _____ .

5. I'm **afraid** of (to) _____ .

6. I'm not **afraid** of (to) _____ .

7. I **feel** _____ .

Two Boyfriends

Reread the dialog "Two Boyfriends" (page 81 of **The Pizza Tastes Great**) before doing the Story Review, Word Review, and Word and Story Review.

DIALOG REVIEW

If the sentence is true, write **T**. *If it's false, write* **F** *and change it to a true statement.*

1. _____ Kelly is a good secretary.
   _____

2. _____ She's pretty and likes to dance.
   _____

3. _____ Mike is her only boyfriend.
   _____

4. _____ Mike and Kelly go to the movies every Saturday night.
   _____

5. _____ Mike and Ray are good friends.
   _____

6. _____ Kelly likes Mike a lot, but she doesn't want to marry him.
   _____

7. _____ She knows she's going to hurt Mike's feelings.
   _____

WORD REVIEW

Complete the sentences with these words.

lawyer	e-mail	hurts	either

1. I love _____. It's so fast and easy to send.

2. You have to study hard to be a _____.

3. I don't like to shop, and my husband doesn't _____.

4. When I know someone doesn't like me, it _____.

answers	mechanic	truth	fair

5. Tell me what happened. I have to know the _____.

6. My wife always _____ the phone.

7. Veronica and I do the same work and get the same pay. That's _____.

8. The _____ says it'll cost $700 to fix our car.

WORD AND STORY REVIEW

Complete the dialog with these words and practice it with a partner.

excellent	busy	filing	fixed
also	fun	soon	however

A New Club

Kelly is Mr. Clark's secretary. Mike calls her at work; they talk about a new club and her car.

Kelly: Good afternoon. Mr. Clark's office.

Mike: Hi, Kelly. Are you _____?

Kelly: Very. _____, for you I have time.

Mike: What are you doing?

Kelly: _____ some letters.

Mike: I want to take you to a new club Saturday night.

Kelly: Great, that sounds like _____.

Mike: It will be; the music is _____.

Kelly: Did you check my car yet?

Mike: Yes, and I _____ the brakes.

Kelly: Good. Any other problems?

Mike: You're _____ going to need new tires.

Kelly: When?

Mike: Not now, but _____.

Kelly: Thanks for your help!

Mike: It's nothing. See you Saturday night.

READING A STORY

Read the story about Karen and Wayne. She's a nurse and he's a doctor.

In Love

Karen is a nurse at a busy hospital. It's not an easy job, but she loves it. She likes to help people and is very understanding. She's always pleasant and kind, and that helps the patients a lot. Karen is 25 and single. But she's not going to be single very long. She's in love with a young doctor who works at the hospital. His name is Wayne.

Wayne is 28. He isn't handsome, but he's very smart and an excellent doctor. He works long hours and doesn't have much time to spend with Karen. But he loves her very much and takes her out to dinner when he has a day off. They plan to get married in May and fly to Puerto Rico for their honeymoon.

WRITING A STORY

Write two paragraphs about a young couple who are single and in love. In the first paragraph, write about the young woman. In the second, write about the young man. You may get some ideas from the story "In Love," but write your own story and give it a title.

Will Kelly Say Yes?

Reread the story "Will Kelly Say Yes?" (page 85 of **The Pizza Tastes Great**) before doing the Story Review, Word Review, and Word and Story Review.

STORY REVIEW

*If the sentence is true, write **T**. If it's false, write **F** and change it to a true statement.*

1. _____ Ray's pay is low.

_____

2. _____ Heavy traffic and wild drivers make his job difficult.

_____

3. _____ On Sunday, Kelly cooks dinner for him.

_____

4. _____ After dinner, Ray and Kelly like to go for a walk.

_____

5. _____ When the weather is bad, they watch TV.

_____

6. _____ Kelly loves and understands Ray.

_____

7. _____ He's rich and handsome.

_____

WORD REVIEW

Complete the sentences with these words.

salary	wind	future	wild

1. Tony's party was a little _____.

2. My _____ is going up next month. I'm very happy.

3. Don't worry about the past. Think about your _____.

4. The _____ is coming from the south. That's why it's so hot.

usually	handsome	hope	nervous

5. Ken isn't _____, but he's very friendly.

6. Grace is _____. She's going to the dentist.

7. I _____ read the newspaper before I go to work.

8. My sister is very sick, but the doctor says there's still _____.

WORD AND STORY REVIEW

Complete the dialog with these words and practice it with a partner.

traffic	eat out	passengers	of course
appetite	polite	tough	heavy

A Big Question

Ray takes Kelly to their favorite restaurant. He asks her to marry him. What is she going to say?

Kelly: This is my favorite restaurant. I love to _____.

Ray: Me too! You know what an _____ I have.

Kelly: How was work today?

Ray: It was _____.

Kelly: Was there a lot of _____?

Ray: No. It wasn't that _____.

Kelly: Were the _____ a problem?

Ray: Yes, most were _____, but some were terrible.

Kelly: Forget about them and enjoy your dinner.

Ray: I will, but first I have a question for you.

Kelly: What is it?

Ray: Do you love me a lot?

Kelly: Yes, I'm crazy about you.

Ray: Will you marry me?

Kelly: _____ I will!

Ray: I have something for you.

Kelly: What a beautiful ring! I love it!

MATCHING

Match the words in Column A with their definitions or descriptions in Column B. Print the letters on the blank lines.

	Column A		Column B
_____	1. mess	**A.**	to ask for in writing
_____	2. may	**B.**	money you must pay back
_____	3. start	**C.**	what birds do
_____	4. apply	**D.**	desire to eat
_____	5. file	**E.**	to begin working
_____	6. fly	**F.**	a person who fixes cars
_____	7. wrong	**G.**	no order
_____	8. loan	**H.**	how much money you make
_____	9. mechanic	**I.**	to put papers in a cabinet
_____	10. salary	**J.**	a person traveling on a bus, train, or plane
_____	11. appetite	**K.**	to be possible
_____	12. passenger	**L.**	not working as it should

SHARING INFORMATION

Discuss these questions with a partner or in a small group.

1. Why is it important to know how to use a computer?
2. How good are you at using computers?
3. How much education does a secretary need?
4. How much money do you think a secretary makes in a year? A mechanic? A bus driver? A nurse?
5. What do you think is a good salary?
6. How important is money to you? (a) very important (b) important (c) not that important
7. What do you hope to be or do in the future?
8. How much education do you need for that?

5

Work and Shopping

On Sale

Reread the dialog "On Sale" (page 91 of **The Pizza Tastes Great**) before doing the dialog and word reviews.

DIALOG REVIEW

If the sentence is true, write **T**. *If it's false, write* **F** *and change it to a true statement.*

1. _____ Lee is wearing a new coat.

   _____

2. _____ Park doesn't like it.

   _____

3. _____ It was very expensive.

   _____

4. _____ It was on sale.

   _____

5. _____ Lee got it at a small store.

   _____

6. _____ Park likes to shop at Sears.

   _____

WORD REVIEW

Complete the sentences with these words.

how much	shop	glad	looks
terrific	price	too	on sale

1. Dave _____ terrible. Is he sick?

2. Debbie likes country music, and I do _____.

3. & 4. Mrs. Barsky is a _____ teacher.

   My son is _____ he has her.

5. _____ was your new bike?

6. The _____ of vegetables goes up in the winter.

7. I'm going to buy these shoes. They look good and they're _____.

8. When do you usually _____?

MISSING LINES

Use the following lines to complete the mini-dialogs.

Where do you like to shop?   Where did you get that book?

Tomorrow morning.   How much was your DVD player?

You look terrific.

1. **Shawn:** When does the sale begin?

    Hana: _____

2. **Shawn:** _____

    Hana: From the library.

3. **Shawn:** _____

    Hana: Thank you.

4. **Shawn:** _____

    Hana: In the department stores at the mall.

5. **Shawn:** _____

    Hana: Two hundred dollars.

A NEW CAR

WORD BANK

Ago means in the past.
Cheap means not costing much; not expensive. *Expensive* is the opposite of *cheap*.

Complete the dialog with these words and practice it with a partner.

careful	cheap	ago	worry	drive	cost

Ben has a new Honda. Liz thinks it looks great. Ben lets her drive it.

Ben: Do you like my new Honda?

Liz: Yes, it looks great. When did you get it?

Ben: Two weeks _____.

Liz: Can I _____ it?

Ben: Sure, but be _____!

Liz: Don't _____. I will.

Ben: Here are the keys.

Liz: Thanks. How much did the car _____?

Ben: Twenty-two thousand.

Liz: That's not bad.

Ben: No, it isn't. New cars aren't _____.

WRITING A DIALOG

Work with a partner and create your own dialog. Give your dialog a title.

_____

A: Do you like my new _____?

B: Yes, it looks _____.

A: _____

B: _____

A: _____

B: _____

A: _____

B: _____

ABOUT HOW MUCH?

About how much do you think these things cost? The clothing is on sale at a department store like Sears or Macy's.

1. A pair of sneakers costs about _____.

2. A dress costs about _____.

3. A man's suit costs about _____.

4. A pair of jeans costs about _____.

5. A man's belt costs about _____.

6. A blouse costs about _____.

7. A skirt costs about _____.

8. A shirt costs about _____.

9. A tie costs about _____.

10. A new small car—for example, a Ford Focus—costs about _____.

A New Dress

Reread the dialog "A New Dress" (page 94 of **The Pizza Tastes Great**) before doing the dialog and word reviews.

DIALOG REVIEW

If the sentence is true, write **T**. *If it's false, write* **F** *and change it to a true statement.*

1. _____ Allison's key is in her handbag.
   _____

2. _____ Adam lets her in.
   _____

3. _____ Allison got a new dress.
   _____

4. _____ Adam is happy his wife got a new dress.
   _____

5. _____ Allison doesn't have many dresses.
   _____

6. _____ The dresses she has aren't in style.
   _____

WORD REVIEW

Complete the sentences with these words.

in style	let	one	full of
closets	wrong	other	dear

1. This TV is OK, but I'm going to buy a better _____.
2. It's a nice house, but the _____ are small.
3. _____ me know what time the party begins.
4. Jessica's math teacher isn't very good, but her _____ teachers are excellent.
5. The baby has a box _____ toys.
6. Don's in the hospital, but we don't know what's _____ with him.
7. Can I help you paint the kitchen, _____?
8. Short hair is _____, but Nancy and I don't like it.

AN HOUR LATE

WORD BANK

Around means about.
Midnight is 12 o'clock at night; the middle of the night.

Complete the dialog with these words and practice it with a partner.

around	won't	safe	tell	sorry	only

Diego is 17. It's one o'clock, and he's coming home from a party. His mother is waiting for him.

Mother: Diego! Come in. Thank God you're _____!

Diego: I'm _____ that I'm a little late.

Mother: A little late? Do you know what time it is?

Diego: _____ twelve-thirty.

Mother: It's one o'clock.

Diego: What time did you _____ me to be home?

Mother: By midnight.

Diego: I'm _____ an hour late.

Mother: An hour is a long time to wait.

Diego: You're right. I _____ be late again.

INTERVIEWING

Ask a partner these questions.

1. May I ask you some questions?

2. What colors do you like to wear?

3. When you buy clothes, are you fast, or are you slow and careful?

4. Do you spend a lot of money on clothes?

5. Do husbands like their wives to dress in style?

6. What are the names of some popular clothing stores?

7. When you shop for clothes, do you shop alone? Who, if anyone, goes with you?

8. In many countries, students wear uniforms to school. Do they wear uniforms in your country?

9. Do you think it's a good idea for students to wear uniforms?

ABOUT ME

Complete these sentences.

1. I like to wear _____.

2. I don't like to wear _____.

3. When it's very cold, I wear _____.

4. When it's hot, I wear _____.

5. When I want to relax, I wear _____.

6. When I go to school (work), I usually wear _____.

7. When I play basketball, I wear _____.

A Cashier

Reread the dialog "A Cashier" (page 97 of **The Pizza Tastes Great**) before doing the dialog and word reviews.

DIALOG REVIEW

If the sentence is true, write **T**. If it's false, write **F** and change it to a true statement.

1. _____ Mark is a cashier at a department store.
   _____

2. _____ He doesn't like his job.
   _____

3. _____ He makes a lot of money.
   _____

4. _____ He's looking for another job.
   _____

5. _____ It's easy to find one.
   _____

6. _____ Ashley tells him to keep looking and he'll get one.
   _____

WORD REVIEW

Complete the sentences with these words.

boring	kinds	should	keep
looking for	another	find	little

1. Letter carriers work in all _____ of weather.

2. Dinner is going to be a _____ late tonight.

3. Nicole is _____ her pen.

4. _____ moving, please.

5. May I have _____ slice of pizza?

6. We _____ pay these bills.

7. The baseball game was _____ .

8. I can't _____ my gloves. Did you see them?

MISSING LINES

Use the following lines to complete the mini-dialogs.

Are you looking for another job?	Why is Courtney so thin?
That won't be easy to find.	He's very nice.
Of course, he's a mechanic.	

1. **Brooke:** What kind of person is Mr. Daniels?

   George: _____

2. **Brooke:** _____

   George: No, I like what I'm doing.

3. **Brooke:** Is Billy good at fixing cars?

   George: _____

4. **Brooke:** _____

   George: She eats very little.

5. **Brooke:** We're looking for a nice house that doesn't cost a lot.

   George: _____

A CARPENTER

WORD BANK

An **ad** (advertisement) is information put in a newspaper to get people
   to buy something or to use a service.

To **build** is to use materials to make something.

A **carpenter** is a person who works with wood.

A **construction company** is a company that builds or fixes houses.

Complete the dialog with these words and practice it with a partner.

there's	build	company	fix	ad	construction

Kayla is a carpenter and she likes her work. She's talking to Greg.

Greg: What kind of work do you do?

Kayla: I'm a carpenter. I work for a _____ company.

Greg: Do you _____ new houses?

Kayla: No, we _____ old ones.

Greg: Do you like your work?

Kayla Sure. But _____ one problem.

Greg: What's that?

Kayla Sometimes the _____ doesn't have any work.

Greg: What do you do then?

Kayla I put an _____ in the newspaper.

Greg: Good idea. People always need carpenters.

WRITING A DIALOG

Work with a partner and create your own dialog. Give your dialog a title.

_____

A: What kind of work do you do?

B: I'm a (an) _____.

A: Do you like your work?

B: _____

A: _____

B: _____

A: _____

B: _____

HOW INTERESTING ARE THESE JOBS?

Read the list of ten jobs. Then circle how interesting each job would be for you.

1	=	not interesting
2	=	not that interesting
3	=	interesting
4	=	very interesting

A.	secretary	1	2	3	4
B.	teacher	1	2	3	4
C.	nurse	1	2	3	4
D.	lawyer	1	2	3	4
E.	computer programmer	1	2	3	4
F.	carpenter	1	2	3	4
G.	auto mechanic	1	2	3	4
H.	salesperson	1	2	3	4
I.	store manager	1	2	3	4
J.	businessman/businesswoman	1	2	3	4

I Hate to Get Up

Reread the dialog "I Hate to Get Up" (page 100 of **The Pizza Tastes Great**) before doing the dialog and word reviews.

DIALOG REVIEW

If the sentence is true, write **T**. If it's false, write **F** and change it to a true statement.

1. _____ Wayne doesn't like to get up in the morning.

   _____

2. _____ He gets up at six-thirty.

   _____

3. _____ He has to be at work by seven.

   _____

4. _____ Wayne thinks Jennifer is lucky.

   _____

5. _____ She owns a restaurant.

   _____

6. _____ Her store opens at nine.

   _____

WORD REVIEW

Complete the sentences with these words.

have to	me too	lucky	hate
until	get up	early	own

1. "I'm hot." "_____. I'm going to open a window."

2. & 3. Mr. and Mrs. Meyer _____ two large houses and have very good jobs. They _____ be rich.

4. If you don't _____ now, you'll be late for work.

5. Megan was in a bad fire. She's _____ to be alive.

6. Eric can't go out and play _____ he does his homework.

7. Most people like onions, but I _____ them.

8. I don't feel well. I'm going to ask to go home _____.

I WORK NIGHTS

WORD BANK

Lazy people hate to work.
A **parking lot** is an area used to park cars.
O'Hare Airport is a very large airport near Chicago.
Really means in fact; actually.
A **security guard** is a person who keeps buildings and areas safe.

Complete the dialog with these words and practice it with a partner.

until	lots	lazy	security guard	spend	really

Andrea hates to get up in the morning. Brett sleeps in the morning; he works nights.

Andrea: I hate to get up in the morning.

Brett: That's a problem I don't have. I sleep all morning.

Andrea: You must be _____.

Brett: Not _____. I work nights.

Andrea: What hours do you work?

Brett: From 11:00 P.M. _____ 7:00 A.M.

Andrea: And what's your job?

Brett: I'm a _____ at O'Hare Airport.

Andrea: That must be interesting.

Brett: It can be.

Andrea: What do you do all night?

Brett: I _____ most of my time checking the parking

_____ .

INTERVIEWING

Ask a partner these questions.

1. May I ask you some questions?
2. How many hours do you usually sleep?
3. Do you think you should get more sleep than that?
4. Do you feel better when you get more sleep?
5. When do you work best? In the morning? In the afternoon? At night?
6. Do you have security guards in your school or where you work?
7. Do you think security guards have a dangerous job?
8. Do they have an interesting job?

ABOUT ME

Complete these sentences.

1. I'm **lucky** because I _____ .
2. I don't **own** a _____ , but someday I hope to have one.
3. I have my **own** _____ .
4. I **spend** a lot of time _____ .
5. I **hate** to _____ .
6. I _____ **lazy**. I _____ .

A Busy Shoe Store

Reread the story "A Busy Shoe Store" (page 103 of **The Pizza Tastes Great**) before doing the Story Review, Word Review, and Word and Story Review.

STORY REVIEW

If the sentence is true, write **T**. *If it's false, write* **F** *and change it to a true statement.*

1. _____ Eddie is in the second grade.

   _____

2. _____ He takes swimming lessons every week.

   _____

3. _____ Mary is a good student and wants to be a lawyer.

   _____

4. _____ Paul and Lindsay own a store that sells men's shoes.

   _____

5. _____ Their store opens at 10:00 A.M. and usually closes at 6:00 P.M.

   _____

6. _____ Paul or Lindsay is always in the store.

   _____

7. _____ Paul is good at working with the children and their parents.

   _____

WORD REVIEW

Complete the sentences with these words.

stay	or	beginning	both
almost	close	together	order

1. & 2. It's _____ to rain.

   Tell Tommy and Lisa to _____ in the house and play.

3. Sharon and Cory like to go to parties _____ .

4. Do you want to watch TV _____ go for a walk?

5. Abdul is _____ six feet tall.

6. Sometimes I _____ clothes by phone.

7. What time does the post office _____?

8. We're _____ hungry. We should stop and eat.

WORD AND STORY REVIEW

Complete the dialog with these words and practice it with a partner.

already	learning	run	count
lessons	especially	next	sell

Getting Big

Jack and Lindsay are friends. They meet at a party.

Jack: How old is Eddie?

Lindsay: He's almost four.

Jack: He must be getting big.

Lindsay: Yes. He's taking swimming _____ and going to nursery school.

Jack: What's he _____ at school?

Lindsay: The alphabet and how to _____.

Jack: That's good. And how old is Mary?

Lindsay: Thirteen. She'll be in high school _____ year.

Jack: I can't believe she's 13 _____.

Lindsay: Yes, and she wants to be a lawyer.

Jack: That's great! Do you and Paul still _____ the shoe store?

Lindsay: Yes, we still _____ shoes.

Jack: How's business?

Lindsay: Fine. We're very busy, _____ on Saturdays.

READING A STORY

Read the story about Anna and Bogdan. They own and run a grocery store.

A Small Grocery Store

Anna and Bogdan are married and have two children, Karolina and Jan. They're from Poland, and they own and run a small grocery store. It's not an easy job. The store opens at six in the morning and closes at eight at night. Anna or Bogdan is always in the store. Their prices are higher than in a supermarket, but people go to their store because it's closer to home. Most people buy only a few things, for example, milk and bread. The store is doing well, but the hours are long.

Karolina is 19, and she's in her first year in college. She lives at home and goes to state college. She likes to study, is very smart, and wants to be a dentist.

Jan is 13 and is in the eighth grade. He's also a good student, but what he really likes are sports. He's a good swimmer and a great basketball player. He plays basketball for his school team.

WRITING A STORY

Write two or three paragraphs about a married couple who came to the United States to live. You may get some ideas from the story "A Small Grocery Store," but write your own story and give it a title.

_____

_____

_____

_____

_____

_____

_____

_____

_____

_____

_____

Quiet and Very Serious

Reread the story *"Quiet and Very Serious"* (page 107 of **The Pizza Tastes Great**) before doing the Story Review, Word Review, and Word and Story Review.

DIALOG REVIEW

*If the sentence is true, write **T**. If it's false, write **F** and change it to a true statement.*

1. _____ Paul gets angry quickly and is very serious.
   _____

2. _____ Lindsay likes to talk and tell jokes.
   _____

3. _____ She gets angry a lot.
   _____

4. _____ Paul and Lindsay often fight about the children.
   _____

5. _____ He shouts at the children and hits them.
   _____

6. _____ She lets the children do anything they want.
   _____

7. _____ She's kind and patient.
   _____

WORD REVIEW

Complete the sentences with these words.

laughing	quickly	angry	smiles
shout	jokes	however	kidding

1. The baby _____ a lot at his mother.
2. I hope you're not _____ at my hat.
3. Jason drives fast. _____, he's never had an accident.
4. There's no need to _____. Talk quietly.
5. Time goes _____ when you're busy.
6. Denise says her father knows the president, but I think she's _____.
7. Vince is _____ at me. That's why he's not coming to my party.
8. I have some new _____ to tell you. I hope you like them.

WORD AND STORY REVIEW

Complete the dialog with these words and practice it with a partner.

fighting	**shout**	**true**	**correcting**
forget	**whatever**	**hit**	**obey**

Too Strict

Lindsay thinks Paul is too strict with the children, and Paul thinks Lindsay's too easy on them.

Lindsay: You're too strict with the children.

Paul: Why do you say that?

Lindsay: Because you're always _____ them.

Paul: Maybe, but do I ever _____ them?

Lindsay: No, but you _____ a lot.

Paul: That's OK.

Lindsay: No, it isn't. You _____ they're only children.

Paul: No, I don't. The problem is you're too easy on them.

Lindsay: That's not _____.

Paul: Yes, it is. You let them do _____ they want.

Lindsay: No, I don't. They listen to me and _____ me.

Paul: Why are we _____ about the children again?

Lindsay: Because we're very different.

Paul: How did we ever get married?

Lindsay: I don't know. That's a good question.

MATCHING

Match the words in Column A with their definitions or descriptions in Column B. Print the letters on the blank lines.

	Column A		Column B
_____	1. nursery school	**A.**	anything
_____	2. full	**B.**	not saying much
_____	3. run	**C.**	they make us laugh
_____	4. whatever	**D.**	where very young children go
_____	5. supermarket	**E.**	to do what someone tells you
_____	6. jokes	**F.**	having many; no more space
_____	7. obey	**G.**	where we buy food
_____	8. correct	**H.**	it's easy to hear when people do this
_____	9. quiet	**I.**	to direct a business
_____	10. shout	**J.**	to tell someone they're wrong

WHAT'S YOUR OPINION?

Give your opinion of each of these statements by circling A, B, or C.

A	=	True
B	=	Not True
C	=	I don't know.

		A	B	C
1.	It's easy to teach nursery school.	A	B	C
2.	It's important for children to go to nursery school.	A	B	C
3.	Most children should watch more TV.	A	B	C
4.	It's difficult for a husband and a wife to run a business together.	A	B	C
5.	Some husbands talk more than their wives.	A	B	C
6.	It's easy to be a good parent.	A	B	C
7.	Many parents shout at their children.	A	B	C
8.	Many parents are too easy on their children.	A	B	C

6

The Weather

A Hot Day

Reread the dialog "A Hot Day" (page 113 of **The Pizza Tastes Great**) before doing the dialog and word reviews.

DIALOG REVIEW

If the sentence is true, write **T**. If it's false, write **F** and change it to a true statement.

1. _____ Hamid and Salimah like the heat.

   _____

2. _____ Hamid wants a cold drink.

   _____

3. _____ Salimah hates to work in hot weather.

   _____

4. _____ The hot weather makes Hamid lazy.

   _____

5. _____ And it makes it easy for Salimah to sleep.

   _____

6. _____ It'll be hotter next week.

   _____

WORD REVIEW

Complete the sentences with these words.

lazy	taste	weather	hates
must	would	cooler	killing

1. I don't want to go for a walk. My feet are _____ me.

2. _____ you like to dance?

3. There's nothing we can do about the _____.

4. Valerie didn't go to school today. She _____ be sick.

5. The potatoes are cold. They _____ terrible.

6. Hakeem _____ to shop.

7. The children are playing in the basement. It's _____ there.

8. Ralph eats a lot, sleeps a lot, and watches a lot of TV, but he doesn't do much. He's
_____.

MISSING LINES

Use the following lines to complete the mini-dialogs.

Why are you watching TV so late?   Please. It tastes good.

Do you want something to drink?   Do I need a jacket?

Next week.

1. **Sandy:** _____

   Jesse: Yes, it's getting cooler.

2. **Sandy:** When's Carlos going to Colombia?

   Jesse: _____

3. **Sandy:** _____

   Jesse: I can't sleep.

4. **Sandy:** Would you like some more turkey?

   Jesse: _____

5. **Sandy:** _____

   Jesse: No thanks. I'm not thirsty.

COLD WEATHER

WORD BANK

No wonder is an expression. It means it's not surprising that.
Out means outside a house or other building.
When a house is cold, you **turn up** the heat. The woman in the picture is turning up the heat.
The **weather report** gives you information about the weather.

Complete the dialog with these words and practice it with a partner.

report	let	heat	clear	wonder	out

Bob and Emma hate cold weather. It's only 20 degrees, and their house is cold too.

Bob: I hate this cold weather.

Emma: Me too! It's only 20° _____ .

Bob: And it's not very warm in the house.

Emma: _____ me check the temperature.

Bob: What is it?

Emma: Sixty-two.

Bob: No _____ I'm cold!

Emma: I'll turn up the _____.

  Bob: Thanks.

Emma: What's the weather _____ for tomorrow?

  Bob: _____ and colder.

Emma: Oh no! I'm moving to Florida.

WRITING A DIALOG

Work with a partner and create your own dialog. Give your dialog a title.

_____

A: I hate this _____ weather.

B: Me too! _____

A: _____

B: _____

A: _____

B: _____

A: _____

B: _____

WORD BUILDING

Add **y** *to these nouns to make them adjectives. Drop the* **e** *in* **ice** *and double the* **n** *in* **sun** *before adding* **y**.

Noun	Adjective	Meaning
rain	_____	lots of rain
snow	_____	lots of snow
ice	_____	lots of ice
sun	_____	lots of sun
cloud	_____	lots of clouds

SENTENCE COMPLETION

Complete these sentences.

1. When it's **sunny**, I like to _____.

2. When it's **rainy**, I like to _____.

3. It must be about _____ **degrees** out.

4. I **would like** to _____.

5. _____ **taste(s)** good.

6. **Next** week I _____.

Not a Cloud in the Sky

Reread the dialog "Not a Cloud in the Sky" (page 116 of **The Pizza Tastes Great**) before doing the dialog and word reviews.

DIALOG REVIEW

If the sentence is true, write **T**. If it's false, write **F** and change it to a true statement.

1. ____ There are some clouds in the sky.

    _____

2. ____ Beth asks what the temperature is.

    _____

3. ____ She loves October, but Todd doesn't.

    _____

4. ____ Fall is the season they like the most.

    _____

5. ____ The weather isn't very good in the fall.

    _____

6. ____ The leaves are beautiful in the fall.

    _____

WORD REVIEW

Complete the sentences with these words.

temperature	favorite	there's	season
leaves	mine	degrees	change

1. _____ a phone in the kitchen.

2. The teacher is going to _____ my seat. I talk too much.

3. Is that your umbrella or _____?

4. The _____ is only 26. You'll need a warm coat.

5. Spring is the _____ in which we get a lot of rain.

6. It's going to be a hot day. It's 80 _____ already.

7. After dinner, I sit in my _____ chair and read the newspaper or watch TV.

8. There are no _____ on the trees in winter.

I LOVE SPRING

WORD BANK
Fresh air is air that is clean and cool. **Grass** is the green plant that covers most yards. **Icy** means covered with ice. To **shine** is to give off light.

Complete the dialog with these words and practice it with a partner.

birds	look	icy	shining	fresh	grass

It's a beautiful spring day. Kim Young and Ho Sook love spring. It's their favorite season.

Kim Young: What a great day!

Ho Sook: It sure is. The sun is _____.

Kim Young: The _____ are singing.

Ho Sook: And there'll be no more snow.

Kim Young: Or _____ roads.

Ho Sook: The _____ will be green soon.

Kim Young: And the flowers will _____ so pretty.

Ho Sook: Are the kids outside?

Kim Young: Yes, they're playing baseball in the park.

Ho Sook: Good. They need the _____ air.

INTERVIEWING

Ask a partner these questions.

1. May I ask you some questions?

2. Do you often watch the weather report on TV? Do you often listen to it on the radio?

3. Describe today's weather.

4. What do you like to do in the summer that you don't do in the other seasons?

5. What do you like to eat in the summer?

6. Do you eat more in the summer, or less?

7. Do you spend much time in the sun?

8. In the summer, many people use sun lotion to protect their skin from the sun. Why should they?

WHAT DO YOU THINK?

What temperature do you consider very cold, cold, cool, warm, hot, very hot? Use the Fahrenheit scale. (Fahrenheit is the temperature scale generally used in the United States.)

1. very cold = _____

2. cold   = _____

3. cool   = _____

4. warm   = _____

5. hot   = _____

6. very hot = _____

SPORTS

Many sports have a special season or seasons. List the season when we usually play each sport. Some sports may have more than one season.

1. baseball   _____

2. football   _____

3. basketball (indoors) _____

4. soccer (outdoors)   _____

5. swimming (outdoors) _____

6. golf   _____

7. tennis (outdoors)   _____

8. skiing   _____

Cold and Windy

Reread the dialog "Cold and Windy" (page 119 of **The Pizza Tastes Great**) before doing the dialog and word reviews.

DIALOG REVIEW

If the sentence is true, write **T**. *If it's false, write* **F** *and change it to a true statement.*

1. _____ It's cold, but there's little wind.
   _____

2. _____ Marina is going to wear her heavy coat.
   _____

3. _____ She's going to the bank.
   _____

4. _____ She's going to mail a package.
   _____

5. _____ Leonid wants ten stamps.
   _____

6. _____ Marina will return in about an hour.
   _____

WORD REVIEW

Complete the sentences with these words.

mail	heavy	wears	windy
out	be back	get	would

1. The Sunday newspapers are very _____.

2. & 3. Is it snowing _____?

   Yes, and it's very _____. That's why it feels so cold.

4. Our sofa is old. We should _____ a new one.

5. I have a birthday card for Mario. I'm going to _____ it today.

6. _____ you answer the phone, please?

7. Ms. Barton usually _____ a suit to work.

8. I have to go to Atlanta, but I'll _____ on Monday.

MISSING LINES

Use the following lines to complete the mini-dialogs.

How many donuts do you want?   I'm sorry, but I can't now. I'm very busy.

What are you wearing to work?   To visit his sister. She's sick.

Donna is in Los Angeles on business.

1. **Carol:** _____

   Gabe: Jeans and a sweater.

2. **Carol:** Where is Fred going?

   Gabe: _____

3. **Carol:** _____

   Gabe: Get me six, please.

4. **Carol:** _____

   Gabe: Do you know when she'll be back?

5. **Carol:** Would you help me clean the garage?

   Gabe: _____

JOGGING

WORD BANK

Exercise is physical activity, for example, walking, running, and riding a bicycle.
When you **nap**, you sleep for a short time.
Really means in fact.
Twice means two times.

Complete the dialog with these words and practice it with a partner.

fun	nap	jog	exercise	twice	should

Tara is going to the park to jog. Jeff doesn't want to go with her. He's lazy.

Tara: Is it windy out?

Jeff: No, not now. Where are you going?

Tara: To the park to _____.

Jeff: Do you jog every day?

Tara: No, _____ a week.

Jeff: Is it _____?

Tara: Not really, but it makes me feel better.

Jeff: I don't get any _____.

Tara: You _____. Do you want to jog with me?

Jeff: No. I'm going to watch TV and take a _____.

Tara: I think you're lazy.

Jeff: Very.

WRITING A DIALOG

Work with a partner and create your own dialog. Give your dialog a title.

_____

A: Where are you going?

B: To the park to _____.

A: Do you _____ in the park often?

B: _____

A: _____

B: _____

A: _____

B: _____

THE POST OFFICE

Answer these questions about the post office.

1. What are some reasons people go to the post office?

    _____

    _____

    _____

    _____

2. Is working in the post office a good job? Explain your answer. _____

    _____

3. Do you think the U.S. Post Office does a good job? Explain your answer.

    _____

4. What's your zip code? _____

5. Do they use zip codes in your country? _____

It's Beginning to Snow

Reread the dialog "It's Beginning to Snow" (page 122 of **The Pizza Tastes Great**) before doing the dialog and word reviews.

DIALOG REVIEW

If the sentence is true, write **T**. If it's false, write **F** and change it to a true statement.

1. _____ Steve likes snow.

   _____

2. _____ He thinks it's pretty.

   _____

3. _____ He has to drive to work.

   _____

4. _____ It's ten miles to his work.

   _____

5. _____ They say it's not going to snow much.

   _____

6. _____ Driving will be dangerous.

   _____

WORD REVIEW

Complete the sentences with these words.

so	how	inches	about
begin	dangerous	hate	far

1. It's very _____ to drink and drive.

2. I walk to school every day. It's not _____.

3. This paper is eight and a half _____ wide.

4. When does class _____?

5. & 6. _____ long is the play?

   It's _____ two hours long.

7. I _____ to drive with Angela. She drives too fast.

8. I'm _____ hungry. I have to get something to eat.

NO SCHOOL TOMORROW

Complete the dialog with these words and practice it with a partner.

fights	shovel	inches	wet	of course	means

It's snowing hard. Driving will be difficult and schools will be closed.

Kevin: We have almost six _____ of snow.

Kristin: You know what that _____?

Kevin: Yes, driving will be difficult.

Kristin: And there'll be a lot of snow to _____.

Kevin: But the kids will be happy.

Kristin: That's right. There'll be no school tomorrow.

Kevin: And the snow is very _____.

Kristin: So it'll be perfect for snowball _____.

Kevin: And for making snowmen.

Kristin: Or snow women.

Kevin: _____.

INTERVIEWING

Ask a partner these questions.

1. May I ask you some questions?

2. Why is jogging good for our health?

3. Do you get much exercise?

4. What kind of exercise do you get?

5. How often do you take a nap? Frequently? Sometimes? Rarely? Never?

6. Are you afraid to drive in the snow?

7. How far do you have to go to get to work or school?

8. How do you get to work or school?

WHEN DO WE USUALLY WEAR IT?

*Next to each word, write **hot** if we usually wear this clothing in hot weather. Write **cold** if we usually wear it when it's cold.*

1. gloves   _____

2. shorts   _____

3. boots   _____

4. T-shirt   _____

5. scarf   _____

6. hat   _____

7. swimsuit   _____

8. long underwear _____

From Santiago to New York

Reread the story "From Santiago to New York" (page 125 of **The Pizza Tastes Great**) before doing the Story Review, Word Review, and Word and Story Review.

STORY REVIEW

If the sentence is true, write **T**. If it's false, write **F** and change it to a true statement.

1. _____ Sandra comes from Santiago, a city in the Dominican Republic.
   _____

2. _____ She lives in Manhattan with her parents.
   _____

3. _____ Her brothers want to stay in the Dominican Republic.
   _____

4. _____ She works in her cousin's grocery store.
   _____

5. _____ She knows very little English.
   _____

6. _____ Americans seem cold to Sandra.
   _____

7. _____ She's going to go back to Santiago.
   _____

WORD REVIEW

Complete the sentences with these words.

if	crying	friendly	cold
almost	sometimes	dream	seems

1. & 2. Erica _____ to be a very nice person.

   She's _____, and I like her a lot.

3. Dinner is _____ ready.

4. I like to _____ that I'm a great actor.

5. _____ you're sick, you should stay home.

6. _____ we play Ping-Pong after school.

7. Sam is very quiet and never says hello to me. He's _____.

8. The baby is _____. I think she's tired.

WORD AND STORY REVIEW

Complete the dialog with these words and practice it with a partner.

uncle	there are	still	grocery
until	stay	owns	go back

No Jobs There for Me

Carlos meets Sandra at a party, and they're talking.

Carlos: Where do you work, Sandra?

Sandra: In a _____ store on Broadway.

Carlos: Do you like your work?

Sandra: No. The hours are too long.

Carlos: What are they?

Sandra: From ten in the morning _____ eight at night.

Carlos: Wow! That's long. Who _____ the store?

Sandra: My cousin.

Carlos: And where do you live?

Sandra: In an apartment with my _____ and cousins.

Carlos: Are your parents _____ in the Dominican Republic?

Sandra: Yes, they live in Santiago.

Carlos: Do they want to come to New York?

Sandra: No, they want to _____ in Santiago.

Carlos: How do you like New York?

Sandra: I don't. I want to _____ to Santiago.

Carlos: Well, why don't you?

Sandra: _____ no jobs there for me.

READING A STORY

Read the story about Juan, a high-school student.

What a Difference!

Juan is 16, and he comes from Lima, the capital of Peru. He lives with his dad and older brother in a small apartment in Philadelphia. He goes to a large public high school. His mom and younger sister still live in Lima, but they're coming to Philadelphia next year. He can't wait to see them again.

At first, Juan didn't like it in Philadelphia. He didn't know anyone at school. He didn't understand English, and the snow and cold were terrible. And of course he missed his mom, his sister, and his friends.

Now it's a year later, and he feels at home in Philadelphia. He has a lot of friends at school. He's getting A's in math and science and B's in English and history. He's one of the best players on the soccer team. His dream is to go to college and become an accountant, and his teachers say he can do it. He's happy. What a difference a year makes!

WRITING A STORY

Write two or three paragraphs about your first year in the United States. You may get some ideas from the story "What a Difference!," but write your own story and give it a title.

Sandra Can't Wait

Reread the story "Sandra Can't Wait" (page 129 of **The Pizza Tastes Great**) before doing the Story Review, Word Review, and Word and Story Review.

STORY REVIEW

If the sentence is true, write **T**. If it's false, write **F** and change it to a true statement.

1. _____ Sandra likes many things about living in the United States.
   _____

2. _____ She sends her parents a money order every week.
   _____

3. _____ Her uncle is teaching her how to drive.
   _____

4. _____ Roberto is 20 years old.
   _____

5. _____ Sandra and Roberto plan to get married in June.
   _____

6. _____ She doesn't like to write, but she calls Roberto every week.
   _____

7. _____ Roberto plans to come to the United States soon.
   _____

WORD REVIEW

Complete the sentences with these words.

sending	money order	yet	besides
every	arrive	hurry	cost

1. I'm going to buy those earrings. They're pretty, _____ they're not expensive.

2. & 3.   When is the president going to _____?

   We're not sure. He isn't here _____.

4. Mark is _____ his girlfriend a dozen roses for Valentine's Day.

5. We have to go now. We're in a _____.

6. I want a _____ for $200, please.

7. Gina goes for a walk _____ afternoon.

8. How much does it _____ to fly from Newark to Los Angeles?

WORD AND STORY REVIEW

Complete the dialog with these words and practice it with a partner.

also	**department stores**	**get married**	**save**
shop	**visa**	**beach**	**soon**

What Do You Like?

Carlos meets Sandra at a party, and they're talking.

Carlos: What do you like about living in the United States?

Sandra: I can _____ money.

Carlos: What else do you like?

Sandra: I like to _____ here.

Carlos: Where do you usually shop?

Sandra: In the big _____.

Carlos: Me too. They have everything.

Sandra: And in the summer, I like to go to the _____.

Carlos: I'm sure that's fun.

Sandra: It is, and I'm _____ learning to drive.

Carlos: Do you have a boyfriend?

Sandra: Yes. His name is Roberto. We're going to _____.

Carlos: Does he live in New York?

Sandra: No, in Santiago, but he's coming here _____.

Carlos: That's great!

Sandra: Yes. He's waiting for his _____.

Carlos: It was nice talking to you. Good luck!

Sandra: Thanks.

MATCHING

Match the words in Column A with their definitions or descriptions in Column B. Print the letters on the blank lines.

	Column A		Column B
_____	1. mine	**A.**	a good place to go in the summer
_____	2. leaves	**B.**	the one after this
_____	3. wear	**C.**	not friendly
_____	4. bodega	**D.**	we need them to send letters
_____	5. beach	**E.**	to want to
_____	6. impossible	**F.**	trees have lots of them
_____	7. stamps	**G.**	my mother's sister
_____	8. next	**H.**	we do this with clothing
_____	9. temperature	**I.**	can't be
_____	10. would like	**J.**	what I own
_____	11. cold	**K.**	it tells us how hot or cold it is
_____	12. aunt	**L.**	a small grocery store

SHARING INFORMATION

Discuss these questions with a partner or in a small group.

1. Do you have any brothers or sisters in your country? If so, are they going to come to the United States?

2. Where can people get jobs if they don't know English?

3. Do you have a dream—something you really want to be or to have? What is it?

4. Are you able to save money?

5. Do a lot of people send money from the United States back to their country? How do they send the money?

6. Can you name some big department stores?

7. Do you have a favorite department store? If so, which one? Why is it your favorite?

8. Why is it expensive to own a car?

7

Sports and Fun

It's Better to Play

Reread the dialog "It's Better to Play" (page 135 of **The Pizza Tastes Great**) before doing the dialog and word reviews.

DIALOG REVIEW

*If the sentence is true, write **T**. If it's false, write **F** and change it to a true statement.*

1. _____ Nicole is still a cheerleader.

   _____

2. _____ She is playing volleyball.

   _____

3. _____ Angela is happy that Nicole is playing basketball.

   _____

4. _____ Jesse doesn't think Nicole should play basketball.

   _____

5. _____ Nicole is a good basketball player.

   _____

6. _____ Her team isn't great, but they win some.

   _____

WORD REVIEW

Complete the sentences with these words.

still	quit	wins	cheerleaders
cheer	lose	better	quite

1. Jennifer is _____ tall.

2. No one wants to _____, but one team has to.

3. The _____ look nice in their new uniforms.

4. Are the children _____ watching TV?

5. I like to play tennis with John, but he usually _____.

6. It's fun to _____ at the games.

7. The weather is going to be _____ tomorrow.

8. I don't want to _____ my job, but I hate it.

MISSING LINES

Use the following lines to complete the mini-dialogs.

No, I quit.   My son is doing well in school.

It's quite good.   How do you feel?

Are you ready to go?

1. **Eric:** _____

   Kathy: Much better.

2. **Eric:** Are you still on the volleyball team?

   Kathy: _____

3. **Eric:** _____

   Kathy: Not yet.

4. **Eric:** _____

   Kathy: Good for him.

5. **Eric:** How's your sandwich?

   Kathy: _____

LOOKING FOR A JOB

WORD BANK

Enough means as much as you need.
Experience is learning that comes from doing something.

Complete the dialog with these words and practice it with a partner.

enough	kind	quit	yet	experience	boring

Chelsea is loking for a job. She wants to work with computers.

Vince: Are you still working at the bank?

Chelsea: No. I _____.

Vince: Was the job _____?

Chelsea: No, but I didn't make _____ money.

Vince: Do you have a new job?

Chelsea: Not _____.

Vince: What _____ of work do you want?

Chelsea: I want to work with computers.

Vince: How much _____ do you have with them?

Chelsea: A lot. I worked with them at the bank.

Vince: I hope you find a job soon.

Chelsea: Thanks.

WRITING A DIALOG

Work with a partner and create your own dialog. Give your dialog a title.

_____

A: Are you still _____?

B: No, I _____.

A: _____

B: _____

A: _____

B: _____

A: _____

B: _____

SHARING INFORMATION

Discuss these questions with a partner or in a small group.

1. Some sports have cheerleaders. Some don't. Which sports usually have cheerleaders? Which sports don't?

2. Do they have cheerleaders in your country? If so, which sports have them?

3. Do you think having cheerleaders at games is a good idea? Explain your answer.

4. Do you think it's fun to be a cheerleader? Explain your answer.

5. It's better to play a sport than to watch one. What are some sports people can still play when they're older?

6. When we play a game, what's more important: to win or to have fun? Explain your answer.

7. Are you good at using computers?

8. Would you like a job where you spend a lot of time working at a computer? Explain your answer.

A Picnic

Reread the dialog "A Picnic" (page 138 of **The Pizza Tastes Great**) before doing the dialog and word reviews.

DIALOG REVIEW

If the sentence is true, write **T**. *If it's false, write* **F** *and change it to a true statement.*

1. _____ Hassan wants to go to a baseball game.

   _____

2. _____ Hassan and Selma are going to a park.

   _____

3. _____ It's about three miles to the park.

   _____

4. _____ The park has picnic tables and a pretty lake.

   _____

5. _____ They're going to bring soda, cookies, and sandwiches.

   _____

6. _____ The kids won't want to go.

   _____

WORD REVIEW

Complete the sentences with these words.

shall	sunny	beautiful	let's
kids	around	bring	far

1. Is the airport _____ from here?

2. I love your garden. It's _____.

3. & 4. Where are the _____?

   Why didn't you _____ them with you?

5. There are only a few clouds in the sky; it's going to be hot and _____.

6. It's 11 o'clock and I'm tired. _____ go home.

7. _____ a million people live in Detroit, Michigan.

8. I'm very hungry. Where _____ we eat lunch?

BEAR MOUNTAIN STATE PARK

WORD BANK

A **hike** is a long walk. To **hike** is to go for a long walk.
A **pool** is a small area of water for swimming.
A **zoo** is a place that keeps animals so people can look at them.

Complete the dialog with these words and practice it with a partner.

zoo	less	hike	get	how about	pool

Gita and Raj are going to Bear Mountain State Park. It has a lot of places to hike.

Gita: What do you want to do on Saturday?

Raj: I don't know.

Gita: Let's go for a _____ with the kids.

Raj: That's a wonderful idea! Where shall we go?

Gita: _____ Bear Mountain State Park?

Raj: Perfect. It has a lot of places to hike.

Gita: And a _____.

Raj: Great! The kids will love the animals.

Gita: And it has a swimming _____.

Raj: How long will it take to _____ there?

Gita: _____ than an hour. It's about 50 miles.

Raj: Good. That's not so far.

INTERVIEWING

Ask a partner these questions.

1. May I ask you some questions?

2. Sandwiches are very popular in the United States, especially for lunch. Are they also popular in your country?

3. Is it better to drink water or soda? Explain your answer.

4. Do you like to hike—to go for long walks?

5. Do you hike much?

6. Do you like to visit zoos?

7. What animals in the zoo are the most interesting? Do you have a favorite?

8. Do you think it's more fun to swim in a pool, in a lake, or in the ocean?

PICNICS AND PARKS

A. *List four or five things people often take on a picnic. Work with a partner.*

1. _____
2. _____
3. _____
4. _____
5. _____

B. *List four or five things people often do on a picnic. Work with a partner.*

1. _____
2. _____
3. _____
4. _____
5. _____

C. *Discuss these questions with a partner.*

1. Do you like sandwiches?

2. What kind do you like? Which is your favorite?

3. What is your favorite soda?

4. Do you drink a lot of soda?

5. Is there a park near your house or apartment? Do you use it much?

Going Skiing

Reread the dialog "Going Skiing" (page 141 of **The Pizza Tastes Great**) before doing the dialog and word reviews.

DIALOG REVIEW

If the sentence is true, write **T**. If it's false, write **F** and change it to a true statement.

1. _____ It's still snowing.
   _____

2. _____ Vicky likes to ski.
   _____

3. _____ Tim wants to go skiing with Vicky.
   _____

4. _____ She says it's safe to drive.
   _____

5. _____ Tim compares driving and skiing.
   _____

6. _____ Vicky tells him not to worry.
   _____

WORD REVIEW

Complete the sentences with these words.

fun	careful	worry	break
deep	has got	storm	over

1. How did you _____ your nose?

2. Brittany _____ a bad headache.

3. Danielle doesn't look well. I _____ about her.

4. Is the pool _____?

5. The game is almost _____, and our team is winning.

6. I like to dance. It's _____.

7. We're going to get a bad _____. We expect 15 inches of snow.

8. Be _____! The floor is wet.

133

MISSING LINES

Use the following lines to complete the mini-dialogs.

Playing in the street is dangerous.　　It's a lot of fun.

My husband is in the hospital.　　Are you serious?

My son got 100 on his history test.

1. **Grace:** _____

   Phil: Don't worry. He'll be OK.

2. **Grace:** Why do you play so much tennis?

   Phil: _____

3. **Grace:** _____

   Phil: That's why the children should go to the park.

4. **Grace:** I'm having lunch with the president of the United States.

   Phil: _____

5. **Grace:** _____

   Phil: Wow! That's great!

COLD WEATHER

WORD BANK

Hockey (ice hockey) is a sport played on ice in which the players try to advance a
  puck and score. (A *puck* is made of hard rubber; it is round and flat.)
To **ice-skate** is to move along on ice using special boots. *Skate* is short for *ice-skate*.
Rough is the opposite of gentle. Hockey is a rough sport.
A **skater** is a person who skates.

Complete the dialog with these words and practice it with a partner.

safe	degrees	hockey	ice-skate	rough	sounds

Pete is happy that it's very cold. He wants to ice-skate. He invites Erin to go with him.

Erin: It's 20 _____ out.

Pete: Great! I'll be able to _____ on the lake.

Erin: That _____ like fun.

Pete: It is. Can you skate?

Erin: A little.

Pete: Why don't you come with me?

Erin: OK. Do you think the ice is _____?

Pete: It must be by now.

Erin: I hope you're right. Are you a good skater?

Pete: Yes, I'm on the _____ team.

Erin: That's a _____ sport.

Pete: I know, but I love it.

WRITING A DIALOG

Work with a partner and create your own dialog. Give your dialog a title.

_____

A: It's going to be cold today.

B: That's good!

A: What's so good about it?

B: I _____.

A: _____

B: _____

A: _____

B: _____

SENTENCE COMPLETION

Complete these sentences.

1. I **have got** _____.

2. It's _____ to **ski**, but it's _____.

3. I'm happy that _____ is **over**.

4. The _____ is very **deep**.

5. I'm **careful** when I _____.

6. Ice hockey is a **rough** sport. _____ and _____ are also rough sports.

7. _____ and _____ aren't rough sports.

Soccer

Reread the dialog "Soccer" (page 144 of **The Pizza Tastes Great**) before doing the dialog and word reviews.

DIALOG REVIEW

If the sentence is true, write **T**. If it's false, write **F** and change it to a true statement.

1. _____ Casimir is going to play soccer.
   _____

2. _____ Ivana also likes soccer.
   _____

3. _____ She never played soccer.
   _____

4. _____ She is going to watch Casimir play.
   _____

5. _____ Casimir thinks he's a great soccer player.
   _____

6. _____ Ivana wants his team to win.
   _____

WORD REVIEW

Complete the sentences with these words.

promised	win	anymore	improving
used to	later	fan	counts

1. Heather is a basketball _____.

2. José _____ to drive us to the airport this afternoon.

3. I have to get back to work. I'll talk to you _____.

4. Education _____ a lot in life.

5. Our football team is very good. We should _____ most of our games.

6. The weather is _____. It's going to be a nice day.

7. & 8. Our son _____ take swimming lessons.
   However, he doesn't take them _____.

COME ON! YOU'LL FEEL BETTER!

WORD BANK

Come on is an expression you use to get someone to do something.
An **excuse** is a reason a person gives for not doing something.
Pace is how quickly or how slowly you do something.
Shape is the physical condition of a person.

Complete the dialog with these words and practice it with a partner.

exercise	who's	excuses	shape	other	pace

Gloria invites Doris to walk with her.

Doris: Where are you going?

Gloria: For a long walk.

Doris: How often do you go for a walk?

Gloria: Every _____ day.

Doris: I should get more _____.

Gloria: Why don't you come with me?

Doris: I'm busy.

Gloria: No _____! Come on! You'll feel better!

Doris: How far do you walk?

Gloria: Three miles at a fast _____.

Doris: You must be in good _____.

Gloria: I am, for someone _____ 65.

Doris: OK, I'll go with you.

Gloria: Good. You can finish your work later.

INTERVIEWING

Ask a partner these questions.

1. May I ask you some questions?

2. Can you ice-skate? Do you ice-skate much?

3. Do you like ice hockey? Did you ever go to a hockey game?

4. Do you ever watch hockey on TV? Do you watch it much?

5. Hockey and football are dangerous sports. Which do you think is more dangerous?

6. Can you name two countries, besides the United States, in which hockey is very popular?

7. Do you think you should get more exercise?

8. Do you feel better after you exercise?

WHAT CAN YOU DO?

Name three or four things you can do. If you can do them well, put a check (✔) between the parentheses.

1. ( ) I can _____.

2. ( ) I can _____.

3. ( ) I can _____.

4. ( ) I can _____.

Name three things you can't do. If you want to learn how to do them, put a check (✔) between the parentheses.

1. ( ) I can't _____.

2. ( ) I can't _____.

3. ( ) I can't _____.

A Vacation

Reread the story "A Vacation" (page 147 of **The Pizza Tastes Great**) before doing the Story Review, Word Review, and Word and Story Review.

STORY REVIEW

If the sentence is true, write **T**. If it's false, write **F** and change it to a true statement.

1. _____ Chris and Jessica are going away for a week.
   _____

2. _____ They're renting a house on a lake north of Miami.
   _____

3. _____ Chris is a carpenter, but he doesn't like his job.
   _____

4. _____ He enjoys the peace and quiet of the country.
   _____

5. _____ Chris and Jessica like to fish.
   _____

6. _____ She's an excellent swimmer.
   _____

7. _____ She spends a lot of time taking people to look at houses.
   _____

WORD REVIEW

Complete the sentences with these words.

building	country	renting	spends
quiet	repairing	peace	excellent

1. The work of the United Nations is to help countries live in _____.

2. The college is _____ a new library.

3. We don't have the money to buy a house, so we're _____ an apartment.

4. Mr. Morales is an _____ history teacher.

5. Hillary is looking for a _____ place to read.

6. When the children go to the _____, they love to look at the animals.

7. My son _____ a lot of time playing video games.

8. Gary is _____ his boat. He takes good care of it.

WORD AND STORY REVIEW

Complete the dialog with these words and practice it with a partner.

sell	**enjoy**	**leaving**	**real estate**
relax	**packing**	**repairing**	**feeling**

Going on Vacation

Jessica is talking to her brother, Nick.

Nick: Why are you _____ your clothes?

Jessica: We're going on vacation.

Nick: Where are you going?

Jessica: To a lake 100 miles north of Miami.

Nick: When are you _____?

Jessica: Tomorrow morning at nine.

Nick: It must be a great _____.

Jessica: Yes, it'll be nice to go swimming and to _____.

Nick: How is your _____ business?

Jessica: Fine, I love to _____ houses, but I need a break.

Nick: I can imagine. What's Chris doing?

Jessica: He's _____ a house.

Nick: Give him my best, and _____ your vacation!

Jessica: Thanks, we will.

READING A STORY

Read the story about Steve and Helen. He works for the United Parcel Service and she's a travel agent.

Going to California

Steve and Helen are at JFK (John F. Kennedy) Airport in New York City. They're married, and they're going to California for two weeks. They're going to stay with Helen's sister, who lives in San Diego. This is their first trip to California, and they're excited. Their plane is going to take off in an hour.

Steve works for the United Parcel Service (UPS). He drives a truck and delivers packages. He likes his job, but he doesn't like to drive in the snow. His salary isn't great, but it's not bad either.

Helen works for a travel agency in New York City. She helps people arrange their vacations and other trips. She's friendly and likes to work with people. She knows the best places to go for a vacation. She's also good at making reservations at hotels and on the airlines. Because of her work, she was able to get free tickets for their trip to California.

WRITING A STORY

Write two or three paragraphs about a married couple who are going on vacation. You may get some ideas from the story "Going to California," but write your own story and give it a title.

_____

_____

_____

_____

_____

_____

_____

_____

_____

_____

_____

No Children This Year

Reread the story "No Children This Year" (page 151 of **The Pizza Tastes Great**) before doing the Story Review, Word Review, and Word and Story Review.

STORY REVIEW

*If the sentence is true, write **T**. If it's false, write **F** and change it to a true statement.*

1. _____ Chris and Jessica's children are going on vacation with them.
   _____

2. _____ They feel a little lonely without their children.
   _____

3. _____ Chris and Jessica are paying a lot to rent their house.
   _____

4. _____ Chris can't cook, so Jessica does the cooking.
   _____

5. _____ After Chris and Jessica do the dishes, they go for a walk.
   _____

6. _____ They walk to the state park, which is less than a mile away.
   _____

7. _____ The trees in the park are pretty, and the air is fresh.
   _____

WORD REVIEW

Complete the sentences with these words.

lonely	so	noise	even
forget	location	stay up	together

1. I'm too tired to _____ tonight.

2. When my daughter is away at camp, I sometimes feel _____.

3. Ryan is rich, but his cousin is _____ richer.

4. This is a good _____ for a restaurant.

5. The dishwasher is making a lot of _____.

6. Kimberly and I like to jog _____.

7. It's hot, _____ I'm going to wear shorts to the picnic.

8. Don't _____ to brush your teeth before you go to bed

WORD AND STORY REVIEW

Complete the dialog with these words and practice it with a partner.

woods	couple	heat	long
away from	few	both	fresh

Swimming and Fishing

Jessica and Chris are talking about their vacation.

Jessica: It's great to get _____ the real estate office.

Chris: And the _____ of Miami.

Jessica: Yes, the air here is _____.

Chris: And the lake is so pretty.

Jessica: What shall we do today?

Chris: Let's go for a walk in the _____.

Jessica: Perfect. The state park is only a _____ miles from here.

Chris: I love _____ walks in the park.

Jessica: And tonight we can play cards with the _____ next door.

Chris: Fine. We _____ like to play cards.

Jessica: Tomorrow I'm going swimming.

Chris: And I'm going fishing.

Jessica: This is going to be a wonderful vacation.

Chris: I think so too.

MATCHING

Match the words in Column A with their definitions or descriptions in Column B.
Print the letters on the blank lines.

	Column A		Column B
_____	1. swimming	**A.**	what many eat for lunch
_____	2. rent	**B.**	you need snow to do this
_____	3. improve	**C.**	a person who works with wood
_____	4. dishes	**D.**	children
_____	5. ski	**E.**	to pay to use something
_____	6. peace	**F.**	a game you play on ice
_____	7. carpenter	**G.**	a long walk
_____	8. hockey	**H.**	we use them to eat on
_____	9. vacation	**I.**	fish are good at this
_____	10. kids	**J.**	quiet and calm
_____	11. hike	**K.**	a time to rest and have fun
_____	12. sandwiches	**L.**	to become better

SHARING INFORMATION

Discuss these questions with a partner or in a small group.

1. Do you think you're a hard worker?

2. What do you do to relax?

3. Do you think it's better to live in a town or a large city? Explain your answer.

4. When you go away for a vacation, do you like to travel to different places or stay in one place?

5. Do you like to sleep late on your vacation?

6. Do you read more or do you read less on vacation?

7. When you're on vacation, do you watch more TV or less?

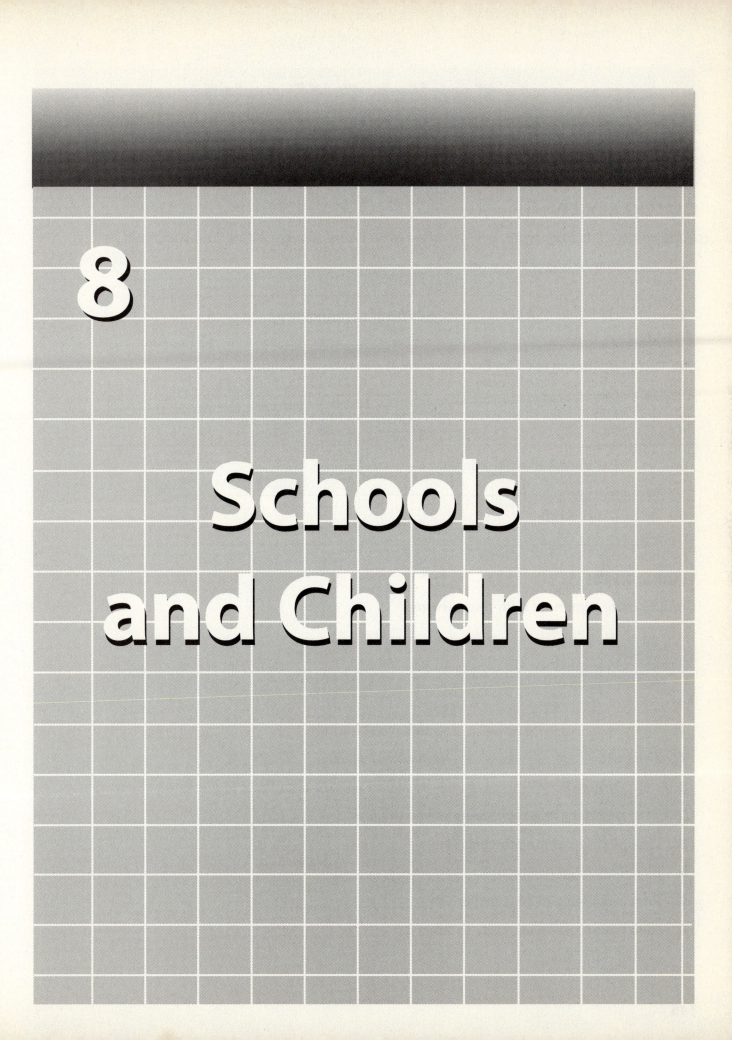

8

Schools
and Children

Is English Difficult?

Reread the dialog "Is English Difficult?" (page 157 of **The Pizza Tastes Great**) before doing the dialog and word reviews.

DIALOG REVIEW

If the sentence is true, write **T**. If it's false, write **F** and change it to a true statement.

1. _____ Marek is going to work.

   _____

2. _____ He thinks English words are difficult to pronounce.

   _____

3. _____ If you can spell an English word, it's easy to pronounce.

   _____

4. _____ Marek tries to be patient and practices a lot.

   _____

5. _____ He doesn't like his teacher.

   _____

6. _____ Class is fun.

   _____

WORD REVIEW

Complete the sentences with these words.

kind	difficult	pronounce	fun
practices	a lot	exactly	learning

1. Can you _____ this word for me?

2. The band _____ twice a week.

3. & 4. Cynthia is _____ to use her computer. She wants to be a

   secretary, and secretaries use computers _____.

5. I'm not afraid of the principal. She's _____.

6. Ivan likes to go fishing. It's _____.

7. Pam is studying to be a lawyer. It's _____.

8. "You have to use a language to learn it." "_____!"

MISSING LINES

Use the following lines to complete the mini-dialogs.

Why not?   No, it's not.

That's good. Was Pedro there?   Do you speak Spanish?

Where are you going?

1. **Kate:** _____

    Pablo: To the movies.

2. **Kate:** I don't like my teacher.

    Pablo: _____

3. **Kate:** _____

    Pablo: Yes, I'm from Ecuador.

4. **Kate:** The party was lot of fun.

    Pablo: _____

5. **Kate:** Is Spanish easy?

    Pablo: _____

STAY IN SCHOOL

WORD BANK
A **diploma** is a document (official paper) that says a person graduated from a school.
To **hire** is to give a job to someone.
The rest means what remains.
The **weekend** is Saturday and Sunday.

Complete the dialog with these words and practice it with a partner.

let	rest	weekends	hire	diploma	quit

Ken is a high school student. He wants to get a full-time job, but his mother says no.

Ken: Mom, I want to get a job.

Mom: On _____?

Ken: No, I want a full-time job, five days a week.

Mom: What about school?

Ken: I want to _____.

Mom: I won't _____ you.

Ken: Why not?

Mom: Who's going to _____ you?

Ken:	McDonald's.
Mom:	Do you want to work there for the _____ of your life?
Ken:	Of course not.
Mom:	Then stay in school and get a _____.

WRITING A DIALOG

Work with a partner and create your own dialog. Give your dialog a title.

_____

A:	What school are you going to?
B:	To _____.
A:	_____
B:	_____
A:	_____
B:	_____
A:	_____
B:	_____

SHARING INFORMATION

Discuss these questions with a partner or in a small group.

1. Do you like school?

2. Why do you like school? Or why don't you like school?

3. Why do some students quit school?

4. What are the problems with quitting school?

5. Do you ever feel like quitting school? If so, why?

6. Do you work after school? If so, what hours do you work?

7. Do you work on weekends? What hours?

8. How difficult is it to go to school and work?

Very Lazy

Reread the dialog "Very Lazy" (page 160 of **The Pizza Tastes Great**) before doing the dialog and word reviews.

DIALOG REVIEW

*If the sentence is true, write **T**. If it's false, write **F** and change it to a true statement.*

1. _____ Melissa is angry at Evan's teachers.

   _____

2. _____ Evan is doing well in math.

   _____

3. _____ Charley thinks Evan is smart.

   _____

4. _____ Evan studies a lot.

   _____

5. _____ His teachers say he's very lazy.

   _____

6. _____ He says he's going to study more.

   _____

WORD REVIEW

Complete the sentences with these words.

promised	surprise	bright	failed
angry	grades	just	lazy

1. Our Spanish teacher is kind, but sometimes he gets _____.

2. When I don't understand my homework, I ask Sara for help. She's _____.

3. My _____ are better this year, and my parents are happy about that.

4. I was _____ today. I didn't do any work.

5. Justin _____ to get his son a bike.

6. I think I _____ my science test. It was very hard.

7. The letter from my cousin was a _____. He never writes.

8. I arrived at work _____ in time.

HISTORY IS IMPORTANT

WORD BANK
To **behave** is to act as we should.   A **mistake** is an error.

Complete the dialog with these words and practice it with a partner.

past	behaving	enough	mistakes	failing	boring

Marissa is not doing well in history. Her dad is explaining why history is important.

Marissa: My history teacher wants to see you.

Dad: If you're not _____, you're in trouble.

Marissa: That's not the problem.

Dad: Well, what is?

Marissa: I'm _____ history.

Dad: Are you studying?

Marissa: Sometimes.

Dad: That's not good _____.

Marissa: But I think history is _____.

Dad: Maybe it is, but it's very important.

Marissa: Why?

Dad: We learn from the _____.

Marissa: What?

Dad: Not to make the same _____.

INTERVIEWING

Ask a partner these questions.

1. May I ask you some questions?

2. Do you think you should study more? Or do you study enough?

3. What are you doing to improve your English?

4. Why is it difficult for an adult to learn a second language?

5. Is it good to know two languages, to be bilingual? Explain your answer.

6. Do you think it's important to study history? Explain your answer.

7. Do you think history is interesting or boring? Explain your answer.

8. Do you know much about the history of the United States?

WHICH SUBJECTS DO YOU LIKE?

List the subjects you're studying in school. Then circle a number next to the subject to show how much you like it.

1	=	I like the subject a lot.
2	=	I like the subject.
3	=	I dislike the subject. (I dislike means I don't like.)
4	=	I dislike the subject a lot.

Subjects

A: _____   1   2   3   4

B: _____   1   2   3   4

C: _____   1   2   3   4

D: _____   1   2   3   4

E: _____   1   2   3   4

F: _____   1   2   3   4

G: _____   1   2   3   4

Too Much Homework!

Reread the dialog "Too Much Homework!" (page 163 of **The Pizza Tastes Great**) before doing the dialog and word reviews.

DIALOG REVIEW

If the sentence is true, write **T**. If it's false, write **F** and change it to a true statement.

1. ____ Dawn thinks she gets too much homework.
   _____

2. ____ She has to do a report for her history class.
   _____

3. ____ The report is due next week.
   _____

4. ____ It will take less than two hours.
   _____

5. ____ Dawn doesn't know how to use the Internet.
   _____

6. ____ Writing the report is a problem.
   _____

WORD REVIEW

Complete the sentences with these words.

too	report	due	takes
at least	couple	Internet	then

1. My daughter spends a lot of time on the _____.

2. It's _____ cold to go for a walk. It's ten degrees out.

3. It _____ me 40 minutes to drive to work.

4. I'm afraid to look at my _____ card.

5. There are _____ 20 students in my class.

6. "I don't want to go to the party. I'm very tired." "_____ don't go."

7. When is the bus _____?

8. Dinner will be ready in a _____ of minutes.

MISSING LINES

Use the following lines to complete the mini-dialogs.

Tomorrow afternoon.   How long does it take you to walk to school?

A report for my boss.   Is Ms. Flores a good teacher?

Do you use the Internet much?

1. **Mayra:** _____

   Adam: Yes, but she gives too much homework.

2. **Mayra:** When do you have to go to the doctor?

   Adam: _____

3. **Mayra:** _____

   Adam: Of course. I send a lot of e-mail.

4. **Mayra:** _____

   Adam: At least 15 minutes.

5. **Mayra:** What are you writing?

   Adam: _____

TOO MANY TESTS

WORD BANK

A **mark** is a score on a test (for example: 75, 90, C, B+). A *grade* and a *mark* are synonyms.
Worst is the superlative of *bad* (*bad, worse, worst*).

Complete the dialog with these words and practice it with a partner.

at least	worst	lucky	tough	mark	how

Both Alex and Lisa have tests tomorrow. They're not happy.

Alex: Tests! Tests! Tests! We get too many tests.

Lisa: You're right. I have a big math test tomorrow.

Alex: You're _____. I have two tests tomorrow.

Lisa: In what?

Alex: English and history.

Lisa: _____ long do you study for a test?

Alex: _____ an hour, usually more.

Lisa: I study two hours if I want a good _____.

Alex: Mrs. Fischer is the _____.

Lisa: Why do you say that?

Alex: She gives a test every week.

Lisa: Are they _____?

Alex: Very.

WRITING A DIALOG

Work with a partner and create your own dialog. Give your dialog a title.

_____

A: Tests! Tests! Tests! We get too many tests!

B: _____

A: _____

B: _____

A: _____

B: _____

A: _____

B: _____

SENTENCE COMPLETION

Complete these sentences.

1. _____ **homework**.

2. I have to _____ a **report** on _____.

3. The _____ is **due** _____.

4. _____ costs **at least** _____.

5. People use the **Internet** to _____

   _____.

6. I use the Internet to _____.

7. It **takes** _____ to _____.

8. _____ a **couple of** _____.

What's a Grant?

Reread the dialog "What's a Grant?" (page 166 of **The Pizza Tastes Great**) before doing the dialog and word reviews.

DIALOG REVIEW

If the sentence is true, write **T**. If it's false, write **F** and change it to a true statement.

1. ____ It costs a lot to go to college.

   _____

2. ____ Brenda's daughter has a grant to go to college.

   _____

3. ____ The grant is paying for everything she needs to go to college.

   _____

4. ____ Brenda's daughter also has a loan.

   _____

5. ____ There's no difference between a loan and a grant.

   _____

6. ____ You have to pay back a grant.

   _____

WORD REVIEW

Complete the sentences with these words.

grant	pay back	proud	difference
government	must	loan	expensive

1. I want to visit Europe, but it's _____.

2. Andrea is _____ of her new car.

3. The children didn't have lunch yet. They _____ be hungry.

4. There's a big _____ between New York City and Washington, D.C.

5. & 6. Jack's father is rich. That's why Jack can't get a _____ to go to college. However, he can get a _____.

7. Some people think our _____ is too big, that it tries to do too much.

8. I'll give you $100, but you have to _____ the money.

I WANT TO GO TO COLLEGE, BUT . . . .

WORD BANK

Aid means help.
Attend means to be present at.
Financial means having to do with money.
A **guidance counselor** is a person who talks to you and helps you to understand and decide things.
Income is the money you receive, especially for the work you do.
When you say **it depends**, it means you're not sure.

Complete the dialog with these words and practice it with a partner.

income	explain	financial	depends	guidance	attend

Alyssa wants to go to college, but her parents don't make a lot of money.

Tyler: Are you going to college?

Alyssa: I want to, but . . .

Tyler: But what?

Alyssa: My parents don't make much money.

Tyler: Then you should be able to get _____ aid.

Alyssa: Where from?

Tyler: The government and the college you _____.

Alyssa: Do you mean the government will help me?

Tyler: Probably. It _____.

Alyssa: On what?

Tyler: Family _____.

Alyssa: I'm going to talk to my _____ counselor.

Tyler: Good. He'll _____ everything.

INTERVIEWING

Ask a partner these questions.

1. May I ask you some questions?

2. What are some jobs that pay well, but that you don't need a college education to get?

3. What are some jobs that you must have a college education to get?

4. Some students go away to college; some live at home. What is good about going away to college?

5. What is good about staying home and going to college?

6. How much do you think it costs to go to a state college for one year?

7. How much does it cost to go to a private college?

8. One good reason to go to college is to prepare for a job. What is another reason to go?

TRUE OR FALSE

If you think the statement is true, write **T**. *If you think it's false, write* **F**.

1. _____ Everyone needs a high school diploma to get a job.

2. _____ People with more education usually make more money.

3. _____ College is expensive, so you have to be rich to go to college.

4. _____ You have to be a very good student to get financial aid.

5. _____ The government helps many students to go to college.

6. _____ Many students get loans to go to college.

7. _____ A loan is usually better than a grant.

8. _____ Many students work part-time to help pay for college.

Long Hours and Hard Work

Reread the story "Long Hours and Hard Work" (page 169 of **The Pizza Tastes Great**) before doing the Story Review, Word Review, and Word and Story Review.

STORY REVIEW

If the sentence is true, write **T**. If it's false, write **F** and change it to a true statement.

1. ____ Young Woo and Sun Ok have two children and live in Philadelphia.

   _____

2. ____ They own a clothing store.

   _____

3. ____ In Korea, Sun Ok had a job outside of her home.

   _____

4. ____ Young Woo works hard in the store but never does any housework.

   _____

5. ____ Sun Ok likes to work in the store.

   _____

6. ____ They go to school at night to learn English.

   _____

7. ____ They speak Korean at home.

   _____

WORD REVIEW

Complete the sentences with these words.

hear	housework	almost	change
listening to	complains	ago	outside

1. & 2. It's _____ six o'clock. Janet is cooking dinner and

   _____ the radio.

3. Where's the dog? Is she _____?

4. Nathan likes his job, but sometimes he _____ about his salary.

162

5. My grandfather doesn't _____ well.

6. I saw Tiffany minutes _____.

7. Sonia usually drinks coffee, but she's having tea for a _____.

8. Marty doesn't like to do _____, but he's a good cook.

WORD AND STORY REVIEW

Complete the dialog with these words and practice it with a partner.

pronounce	hard	own	understand
sell	sounds	close	taking care of

Is the Store Doing Well?

Young Woo is talking to his friend Ling Soo.

Ling Soo: Good to see you again!

Young Woo: And it's nice to see you!

Ling Soo: How's everything?

Young Woo: Fine. Sun Ok and I _____ a store now.

Ling Soo: What kind of store?

Young Woo: We _____ fruit and vegetables.

Ling Soo: And where's Sun Ok?

Young Woo: She's home; she's _____ the children.

Ling Soo: Is the store doing well?

Young Woo: Very. But it's _____ work.

Ling Soo: You must work long hours.

Young Woo: Yes, we open at 8:00 A.M. and _____ at 9:00 P.M.

Ling Soo: And how's your English?

Young Woo: Better. I _____ everything I hear.

Ling Soo: That's great!

Young Woo: Yes, but English words are hard to _____.

Ling Soo: I know. I still have problems with the *l* and the *r* _____.

READING A STORY

Read the story about Akira and Mariko. He works for a bank, and she stays home to take care of their children.

Akira and Mariko

Akira and Mariko are married and have two children, Kenji and Yoko. They're from Japan and live in Fort Lee, New Jersey. Their home is only a few minutes from the George Washington Bridge. Akira is the supervisor of the loan department in a bank in Fort Lee. Many of the people who use the bank are Japanese. Akira has an accent, but he speaks English very well.

Mariko stays home and takes care of Kenji and Yoko. Kenji is eight and in the third grade. He loves school and does very well, especially in science. He also loves computers and all kinds of electronic games. On Saturday, he goes to a special school where he learns to read and write Japanese. Someday the family may return to Japan, and Kenji wants to know Japanese well.

Yoko is only three years old, but she goes to a nursery school three days a week. She likes to draw and to paint, and to play with her friends. She speaks Japanese at home and English at the nursery school. She's already bilingual.

WRITING A STORY

Write two or three paragraphs about a married couple and their two children who come to the United States to live. You may get some ideas from the story "Akira and Mariko," but write your own story and give it a title.

_____

_____

_____

_____

_____

_____

_____

_____

Excellent Students

Reread the story "Excellent Students" (page 173 of **The Pizza Tastes Great**) before doing the Story Review, Word Review, and Word and Story Review.

STORY REVIEW

*If the sentence is true, write **T**. If it's false, write **F** and change it to a true statement.*

1. _____ Schools in the United States and Korea are almost the same.

   _____

2. _____ In Korea, children write down what the teacher says and study it.

   _____

3. _____ In the United States, children seem to do what they want in school.

   _____

4. _____ Tae Ho and Soo Jin's ideas and feelings are almost completely American.

   _____

5. _____ They learn the Korean language at home.

   _____

6. _____ Tae Ho likes to play baseball, but he never helps his parents.

   _____

7. _____ Soo Jin is in the second grade and reads well.

   _____

WORD REVIEW

Complete the sentences with these words.

business	facts	best	feelings
way	half	pay attention	ideas

1.–3. Ms. Romano is one of the _____ teachers in the school.

   She has a lot of new _____, and the students like the

   _____ she explains things.

4. I can't answer your question now. I have to study the _____ first.

5. When the president speaks, people _____.

6. Leo is in the real-estate _____. He sells houses.

7. It was a difficult test. Only _____ the class passed.

8. Sometimes I can't control my _____.

WORD AND STORY REVIEW

Complete the dialog with these words and practice it with a partner.

lessons	**worry**	**engineer**	**fresh**
seem	**excellent**	**respect**	**second**

Learning a Lot

Young Woo is talking to his friend Ling Soo.

Ling Soo: How are Tae Ho and Soo Jin doing in school?

Young Woo: Fine. They're _____ students.

Ling Soo: Does Tae Ho still want to be an _____?

Young Woo: Yes, and he does very well in math.

Ling Soo: And how old is Soo Jin?

Young Woo: She's seven and in the _____ grade.

Ling Soo: I know she loves school.

Young Woo: Yes, and she also takes piano _____ every week.

Ling Soo: What do you think of the schools in the United States?

Young Woo: They're very different.

Ling Soo: How?

Young Woo: In Korea, students have more _____ for teachers.

Ling Soo: That's right; they're never _____ in school.

Young Woo: In the United States, students _____ to do what they want.

Ling Soo: But your children are learning a lot.

Young Woo: True, but we _____ about them.

MATCHING

Match the words in Column A with their definitions or descriptions in Column B. Print the letters on the blank lines.

	Column A	Column B
_____	1. diploma	**A.** what teachers give
_____	2. quit	**B.** to act the way we should
_____	3. boring	**C.** help
_____	4. hire	**D.** all that we need
_____	5. mistake	**E.** cleaning, doing dishes, making beds
_____	6. aid	**F.** what we get when we graduate
_____	7. close (verb)	**G.** to give a job to
_____	8. housework	**H.** what we hear
_____	9. sound	**I.** not interesting
_____	10. lessons	**J.** to shut
_____	11. enough	**K.** an error
_____	12. behave	**L.** to stop doing something

SHARING INFORMATION

Discuss these questions with a partner or in a small group.

1. How much housework do you do?
2. Do you think housework is boring?
3. Do you understand most of what you hear on TV?
4. Does watching TV help you to learn English?
5. What language do you usually speak with your friends?
6. Are teachers stricter in your home country or in the United States?
7. Do you think students learn more in school in your home country or in the United States?
8. Do you think parents worry a lot about their children?

Word List

The words used in the sentence and dialog completion exercises and in the matching exercises are listed below.

A

a lot *5, 35, 52, 148*
a lot of *68*
about (around) *68*
about (on the subject of) *17*
across *63*
ad *91*
afraid *71*
again *5*
age *45*
ago *84, 162*
aid *160, 167*
all *3*
all right *58*
almost *40, 96, 162*
alone *18*
already *97*
also *75, 123*
always *2, 15, 62*
angry *99, 152*
anniversary *52*
annoy *38*
another *6, 34, 40, 89*
answer *75*
any *9*
anymore *137*
anything *48*
appetite *78, 79*
apply *68, 79*
appointment *28*
around (about) *87, 130*
arrive *122*
at least *155, 157*
at night *8*
attend *160*
aunt *124*
awake *8*
away from *144*

B

bakery *48, 59*
be back *112*
be in trouble *69*
beach *123, 124*
beautiful *130*
because *17*
begin *43, 96, 114*
beginning (noun) *42*
behave *153, 167*

belong *37, 40*
besides *122*
best *58,165*
better *25, 43, 126*
bill *35, 40*
bird *110*
birthday *45*
bit *26, 40*
bodega *124*
boring *89, 128, 153, 167*
born *38*
both *17, 19, 96, 144*
brave *55*
break *133*
briefcase *51, 59*
bright *152*
bring *130*
build *91, 140*
business *165*
busy *5, 19, 75*
buy *18*

C

calorie *15*
camera *52*
can *5*
cap *6*
careful *15, 84, 133*
carpenter *91, 145*
cash *68*
cell phone *3*
change *57, 58, 109, 162*
cheap *84*
check *65*
cheer *126*
cheerleader *126*
chocolate *9*
clear *106*
climb *66*
close (near) *69*
close (shut) *96, 163, 167*
closet *86*
clothes *18*
cold (adjective) *119, 124*
cold (noun) *25, 40*
collect *38*
come on *138*

company *91*
compare *38*
complain *162*
computer *55*
construction *91*
cook *2*
cooler *104*
correct (verb) *101*
cost *68, 84, 122*
count (numbers) *97*
count (to be important) *137*
country *140*
couple (few) *144, 155*
couple (two people)
cousin *45, 59*
cry *119*

D

dangerous *119*
darn it *119*
dear *119*
deep *119*
degree *119*
department store *35, 123*
depend *160*
dessert *9*
diet *14*
difference *159*
different *15, 51, 159*
difficult *148*
dining room *3*
dinner *2*
diploma *150, 167*
dirty *62*
drive *22, 49, 84*
due *42, 155*

E

e-mail *155*
early *15, 23, 93*
eat out *78*
either *74*
else *48*
engineer *166*
enjoy *141*
enough *128, 153, 167*
especially *97*
even *143*

every *25, 54, 122*
exactly *148*
excellent *12, 75, 140, 166*
excited *72*
excuse (noun) *138*
exercise *114, 138*
expensive *35, 40, 52, 159*
experience *128*
explain *160*

F

fact *165*
fail *152, 153*
fair *75*
fall *66*
fan *137*
far *69, 114, 130*
fast *14*
favorite *15, 19, 58, 109*
feel *25, 32, 55*
feeling *141, 165*
fever *28*
few *18, 144*
fight (noun) *117*
fight (verb) *18, 101*
file *75, 79*
financial *160*
find *89*
find time *34*
finish *35*
first *37*
fish *11*
fix *75, 91*
flat *65*
flu *32*
fly *71, 79*
foolish *71*
forget *101, 143*
fresh (air) *110, 144*
fresh (person) *166*
friendly *18, 119*
full *101*
full of *86*
fun *75, 114, 133, 148*
future *77*